Praise for

LIVING LIFE BOLDLY

Ted Roberts combines Marine-styled discipline with solid biblical teaching. It is spiritual basic training at its finest!

ROBERT ANDRESCIK
EDITOR, *NEW MAN* MAGAZINE

There is the sound of rushing wind coming out of Oregon; a cocky, swashbuckling fighter pilot turned pastor has fallen in love with Jesus. Throw away the programs and quit playing church; stop doing the "have to's" and respond to the "want to's" of a grateful heart. In *Living Life Boldly,* Ted Roberts speaks in a tongue we can all understand.

JAY CARTY
COAUTHOR, *COACH WOODEN ONE-ON-ONE*
FOUNDER, YES! MINISTRIES

An incredibly vital part of releasing your God-given dreams is to balance it with pure discipleship. The two go hand-in-hand. Ted Roberts leads us simply and powerfully through one of Jesus' favorite topics: living life boldly by following in His steps. Start today!

WAYNE CORDEIRO
AUTHOR, *DOING CHURCH AS A TEAM* AND *THE DREAM RELEASERS*
PASTOR, NEW HOPE CHRISTIAN FELLOWSHIP
OAHU, HAWAII

Ted Roberts is an instrument in the hand of God to help questing hearts set their life course with clarity. This book gives understanding of life's purpose and how to find life's fulfillment by knowing the ways of the Life-Giver. Just as Ted's earlier book leads to freedom, this one points to fruitfulness.

DR. JACK HAYFORD
AUTHOR, *LIVING THE SPIRIT-FORMED LIFE*
FOUNDING PASTOR, THE CHURCH ON THE WAY
CHANCELLOR, THE KINGS' COLLEGE AND SEMINARY

LIVING LIFE
BOLDLY

TED ROBERTS

Regal

From Gospel Light
Ventura, California, U.S.A.

ACKNOWLEDGMENTS

My deepest heartfelt thanks:

To Diane, who loved me into the Kingdom and stole my heart from the first day I saw her.

To my kids, Nikki and Bryan, who taught me the heart of the Father and forgave me so freely like the Son.

To Roy Hicks, Jr., who spoke so prophetically into my life; to Butch Plummer, who showed me what a loving pastor looked like; and to Jack Hayford, who encouraged me to the core of my being.

And to the precious flock of East Hill Church, who challenged me to new heights in Christ and became the extended family I never had.

SCRAMBLED EGGS AND GLORY

I served as an accident investigator in the military. I remember one incident involving a fighter aircraft that ran directly into the side of a mountain. This isn't too unusual, but in this case, there appeared to be no reason for the crash.

Yes, the pilot did experience electrical failure and he was using a backup altitude indicator and compass, but the man had extensive flying experience and was very familiar with the approach to the airfield.

The weather really wasn't much of a factor at all. All the pilot had to do was penetrate a layer of clouds a couple thousand feet thick. The visibility and ceiling below the clouds were excellent. Yet he managed to slam into the side of a mountain. Eventually, we figured out what had happened.

The pilot was flying a type of aircraft I had spent a lot of time in. I knew from experience that there is absolutely no room in the cockpit to store things. If you go on a cross-country flight, you store your clothes and other gear in a drop-tank-style luggage container.

The pilot had just been promoted to what is called a field grade rank. This means you get to wear all those "scrambled eggs"—gold embroidered oak leaves, really—on the front of your hat, or as the military says, "your cover."

Apparently, the pilot didn't want to risk getting his new bejeweled hat dirty by putting it in the drop-tank container. So he took it with him in the cockpit and put it the only place he could—on top of the instrument panel, next to the standby compass. The metal in the hat totally distorted the compass headings, and he was forced to rely on the standby compass, which resulted in his flying right into the mountain.

JESUS KNOWS BEST

In life there are moments when someone close to us succeeds and we don't, or when God apparently reaches right over us to honor someone else. Moments like these can really pull us off course in life. Yet such moments provide some of the deepest revelation about who we are and whom we are really serving in life.

Remember King Saul's son, Jonathan? Every day of his life he probably heard his dad say, "Someday, Son, all of this is going to be yours. The palace, the servants and the army—resources beyond your wildest imagination. It is going to be all yours."

The young man was set for life until a shepherd boy named David decided to take off Goliath's head. In an instant, the affections of Israel were transferred from the House of Saul to the House of David. Talk about some harsh realities that should have thrown Jonathan's soul off course! God apparently reached right over him to bless David.

But Jonathan didn't respond in a competitive or hostile way. In fact, the Bible tells us that "Jonathan loved David as much as he loved himself" (1 Sam. 20:17, *NLT*). What an amazing response!

Jonathan understood that God loves us equally but doesn't treat us the same. Now that may sound strange to you, but it is true. No loving dad will treat his kids exactly the same, because what works for one child may not work for another. This is why every father will hear comments such as, "How come they can do that and I can't?" Father God hears comments like that all the time.

When we ask such questions, we simply don't realize that we are handcrafted by God for a specific purpose. Remember this: *No one can beat you at being you,* so there is no need to compete in the kingdom of God.

Anytime you see God promoting or blessing someone near you, it is not just for their good but also for yours. We are all part of the same combat team. Unfortunately, Jonathan's father, King Saul, never figured that out and eventually died a pitiful, angry man as jealousy corroded his soul.

THE RACE IS ON

I have counseled a lot of Sauls through the years who struggle with who is going to be "king." Jonathan, like David, decided to let the Lord be his King. That attitude releases a marvelous thing in a person's life—a generous heart.

That is precisely what this book is about. For such a time as this, God has placed a desire in your heart to really grow in Christ—a passion that may not be fully developed yet, but it is there and can't be denied. That is why you picked up this book. My prayer is that the words printed on the following pages— words that I have agonized over for the past year—would ignite your soul. I sincerely pray that you won't be the same by the time you reach the final chapter and honestly assess your heart.

I fervently pray that this book *explodes* in your heart and soul, tearing apart all of the false comfort zones you may have constructed in your heart and soul. There is nothing wrong with comfort, but these days there is an outcry for radical disciples of Christ, folks who have so tasted of the grace of God that they really don't care about title, position, prestige or power. Sure, those things may twitch the compass of our soul at times, but they never set our course for long. In many ways, the organized Church has gotten way off course. Yet the Church is the only ultimate hope for our hurting and broken world. Therefore, it is time for us to become truly pure-hearted disciples of Christ, to boldly step forward—not fighting for control of some institution or for position but gladly laying down our lives for Christ. We must fall so in love with the Savior and be so moved by His love for us that our lives once again captivate the hungry hearts of a profoundly lost world. Get ready for the adventure of a lifetime—the call to a pure-hearted discipleship!

CHAPTER ONE

BUCKAROO'S CHALLENGE

The Call for Pure-Hearted Disciples

I must have shifted the materials on the conference table in front of me a dozen times. What I was about to do tied me in knots. It was worse than facing a surface-to-air missile or anti-aircraft fire, or finding myself in the middle of the kind of in-flight emergency that would have had me nearly swallowing my oxygen mask.

What could hit me like this? My very first attempt at speaking publicly for Christ.

I had deliberately chosen the squadron briefing room. After all, I was in my element there. During the previous years, I had given numerous safety briefs and lectures to groups of flight students and instructors in this very room. Churches felt strange and troubling to me, so I didn't want to risk speaking in a "religious" setting. Here I felt as comfortable and in control as possible, given the daunting task before me. Being in control was still critical for me, since Christ had just begun His healing work in my life. Even though I had sense enough to realize that Jesus was the only One really in control, I still felt a rumbling tension within my soul.

The session was nothing more than a simple Bible study that I had decided to have at the squadron. I wanted to grow in my faith, but I couldn't make sense out of church. The church members didn't speak my language, and they also didn't struggle with the same stuff I dealt with on a daily basis. I decided to take the bull by the horns and conduct my own Bible study.

One by one the men sauntered into the room—some in flight suits, some in uniforms and some even in civvies. Most of them were flight students, so I looked forward to sharing with them without the usual instructor-student formality. I glanced down at my outline. I had prepared it from the few sermons I had heard and what little I had learned from my own Bible reading, which ironically made me a biblical scholar compared to the pilots in front of me.

Then Buckaroo entered the room! I know my jaw must have dropped. He swaggered to the far end of the table and flopped in a chair, his flight suit unzipped down to his belly button as usual.

If anyone's call sign fit perfectly, it was Buckaroo's. He was challenging and navy to the core. He took great delight in harassing me for my Marine Corps spit and polish. Nothing was off-limits to him. He had a caustic vocabulary that fed off some of the wickedest humor known to man. Yet I respected the man because once he climbed into the cockpit, he was incredible. He could fly the plane to the absolute edge of the envelope and even toy with it there despite its violent and bucking protest; thus, the name Buckaroo. We had gone head-to-head in several mock dogfights, and the results were never conclusive but always interesting. We had pushed each other to the razor's edge of our abilities and I think in the process gained a mutual respect for one another.

I tried to ignore Buckaroo's piercing stare as I began to walk through the preliminaries of our time together. But just as I launched into my much-rehearsed presentation of the book of Romans, Buckaroo interrupted me midsentence: "Hey, I've got a question," he shot.

Every eye turned toward him as he grabbed the spotlight as usual, but this time there was an honest quest in his words:

Let me tell you about something that happened to me just before I finished my last tour of duty in 'Nam. It was a night carrier launch, and I had a max load for a heavy mission up north. They fired me off the starboard catapult, but about halfway down the deck something went wrong. I found myself going sideway in a violent yaw, and I knew I wasn't about to get airborne flying sideway. I initiated the ejection sequence and blasted out of the plane just before it tumbled into the sea. Everything worked as advertised. I had a good chute that slowed me down enough so my impact with the water didn't break anything, but it still rung my bell. Somehow I managed to fight my way to the surface, get clear of the chute and inflate one side of my flotation gear. I was feeling pretty good about being alive and in such great shape when I realized I had a really *big* problem. The carrier was steaming straight at me doing 30 knots! There was no way they could get the carrier turned away when I was directly in its path. I waved my hands frantically as it roared toward me, which is kind of hilarious now that I think about it. It ran right over the top of me! I felt myself bouncing along the side of the hull like a Ping-Pong ball.

By now everyone in the room leaned forward in their chair, hanging on every word. I thought to myself, *There is no way this guy could have lived through that. He has got to be pulling our leg.*

Then he got my total attention.

"At some point," he continued, "I passed out of my body; it was like I was watching myself rolling, twisting and tumbling along the length of the carrier. I thought about my wife and a lot of other things.

"Then I passed back into my body as I was gyrating through the screws at the stern of the ship and popped to the surface. The compression of passing near the propellers had broken one of my eardrums and the pain was intense. Fortunately, after a short time in the water, one of the escorting destroyers picked me up."

Buckaroo paused for a moment, fixed his gaze on me and said, "I know there is a God; otherwise I wouldn't be sitting here tonight. But, Ted, tell me who this Jesus Christ is and why I should be interested in Him."

I can't remember exactly what I said to Buckaroo that evening. I am sure it wasn't very profound, but it apparently made sense to him because he eventually said yes to Christ. More important, he gave me a great gift that night. His question birthed something in my heart—something of the kingdom of God that I have never forgotten. I heard the honest cry of the human heart. After 20-plus years of ministry, I have come to realize everyone has a Buckaroo story of some sort. Most likely it isn't as dramatic as being keelhauled by an aircraft carrier, but every person has received a love note from the Father at some point in their life prior to saying yes to Christ.

> *Every person has received a love note from the Father at some point in their life prior to saying yes to Christ.*

In years of counseling, pastoring and caring for hurting folks, I have never known anyone whom God isn't reaching out to and touching with His grace—not one whom God the Father isn't passionately pursuing.

WHAT IS THE ROLE OF THE CHURCH IN PURE-HEARTED DISCIPLESHIP?

Unfortunately, in our day and age, a staggering number of folks don't understand who Christ truly is or His deep passion for them. Recently after one of our midweek services, which we direct toward individuals who have already decided to follow Christ, a young lady spoke to me.

"Pastor Ted," she said, "I just love the services here at East Hill. I enjoy hearing you speak, but who is Jesus Christ, and why is He so important to you?"

Many might find such questions rather hard to believe given all the radio, television and other media ministries directed toward evangelism. It is unthinkable that someone wouldn't know who Jesus Christ is! However, if you look at the objective statistics, the *vast majority* of people who watch, listen or are affected by such ministries are Christians, not unbelievers. It is speaking to the already convinced.

Unchurched folks in America don't feel they *need* God very much. They tend to be individuals who have made some headway in life. Their driven lifestyle has left them frazzled and overextended but not necessarily hungry for Christ.[1] The number of unchurched people has grown steadily in the last 50 years in America, and the main reasons they give for not attending church usually revolve around two issues. First, they don't think it is worth the time. Despite the fact that they may be overextended and struggling with relationships, they do not automatically think that Jesus, the Bible or Christianity will help them overcome their difficulties. We live in a post-Christian society.[2]

Second, an increasing number of people choose to live disconnected from any church because they find churches irrelevant to their world and needs.[3]

Clarity in the Midst of Confusion

The Church must begin to grasp Christ's strategy for America, because frankly, things are getting desperate in our land. The unchurched in our land have now become the largest mission field in the English-speaking world.[4] The Western world is also the only major segment of the world's population in which Christianity is not growing.[5]

The problem goes much deeper than just a decline in the number of individuals attending church. There is a severe problem with the faith of many who do attend church. Presently, fewer than half (44 percent) of all born-again adults are convinced there is such a thing as absolute moral truth.[6] This belief partially explains why atheists are less likely to become divorced than Christians in America today.[7]

To complete the grim picture, the United States now leads the industrialized world in the percentage of single-parent families, abortion rates, sexually transmitted diseases and the size of the prison population per capita.[8]

All of these sad statistics do not mean that there isn't a spiritual hunger in our land. Between 1989 and 1998, the Muslim population in the United States grew by 25 percent so that no major American city, including those in the Bible Belt states, is without an Islamic teaching center. Islam has become the second-largest religious group, superseding Judaism.[9] Buddhism is growing nearly three times as fast as Christianity in America.[10] The second fastest-growing religion in North America is Hinduism.[11] These statistics are not just numbers; they represent people who truly matter to God. The present-day Church is deeply confused about its calling; as a result, our nation is in a gut-wrenching state of spiritual confusion.

Confused in Its Calling

This isn't the first time the Church has been confused about God's priorities in its calling. One of the most significant turning points in the book of Acts, outside the Day of Pentecost, was the conflict that erupted over the question of whether the gospel should be spread outside the confines of Judaism. That discussion seems ridiculous to us today, because we enjoy the benefits of the gift of wisdom God gave James, the pastor of the church in Jerusalem:

> When they finished, James spoke up: "Brothers, listen to me. Simon has described to us how God at first showed his concern by taking from the Gentiles a people for himself. It is my judgment, therefore, that we would not

make it difficult for the Gentiles who are turning to God" (Acts 15:13-14,19).

Once you read through the full discussion found in Acts 15, you realize those who were opposed to the Gentiles hearing the good news didn't like how the Gentiles acted and saw themselves as spiritually superior. They probably said something like, "We can't let the Gentiles in because they don't look and act like us. Their hair is different and they wear strange clothes. Besides, they are not very godly." Sadly, similar behaviors and attitudes are prevalent in today's Church.

Realization of Its Godly Calling

We don't have many outside speakers at East Hill because of the rather unique way we do things. It is not that we are closed to outside influences, but it can be rather hard on the speakers. During the review session following the first service, I faced a dilemma. This *very distinguished* speaker had made an off-hand joke about homosexuals. I was waiting for an opportunity to bring up the subject to suggest he avoid such comments in the remaining services. Before I could address the issue, a staff member turned to the speaker and with a great deal of grace and gentleness in his voice said, "Sir, the joke you made about homosexuals doesn't fit with our calling. Those folks are important to us. They need Christ just like we do. God is bringing them to East Hill, and we need to honor that. It doesn't matter if our attendees are homosexuals, prostitutes or powerful people in the community. If they are seeking God, there is a place of honor for them here." Tears came to my eyes. That staff member wasn't confused at all about God's strategy and plan for our land—to reveal to every tongue, tribe and nation God's priority and outrageous love for each and every individual.

One of the most prized gifts I have ever received is proudly displayed in my office—a teddy bear wearing a little flight jacket and goggles. It came with an incredible note written by a former prostitute who walked into East Hill one weekend, met Christ and totally turned her life around. She is married now with two kids and follows Christ with all her heart. Previously, she had been into everything from New Age practices to Buddhism. She has now become a powerful spokesperson for Christ. She is not the only one. Recently, we started a new-believers group for exotic dancers because so many of them started showing up to our services and responding to Christ. We started the group so that they would have a great place to celebrate their new life. I don't mean to be presumptuous, but I suspect that in many congregations they would have told this former prostitute, "You have to clean up your life, you know! You have to develop into a certain kind of person."

But that is not what the father did with his prodigal son in Luke 15. Right up front he threw a party. *True repentance follows grace. And forgiveness precedes repentance.* Heartfelt repentance and conversion occurred for the son only after the party. I would have loved to have been sitting around the breakfast table the next morning. I think the son would have said something like this to his father: "Dad, I want to go back to the far country. I told everyone you were a terrible father. I need to go back and correct that. I need to let those I left behind know what a great and gracious father you really are." The son would not have been confused in the slightest about his father's priorities—about his father's outrageous love for him. The prodigal son would have known exactly what to say to Buckaroo, because he had been keelhauled by his own foolish choices in life. At some point everyone will be foolish apart from Christ. And if they do not discover God's amazing love and redemption in this process, they will miss the greatest adventure available to any man or woman living—life with a determined intimacy with their Savior—a pure-hearted discipleship.

WHAT IS THE CONTINUING CHALLENGE?

Once we stop to think about it, we shouldn't be puzzled by the confusion in American churches today. It always has been a continuing challenge to *keep* the first thing the first thing. In the first few chapters of Revelation, the risen Christ is evaluating and challenging a group of churches in Asia Minor (present-day Turkey). John the Beloved had invested his life in these people, so it is appropriate that he uniquely heard Christ's words for them:

> To the angel of the church in Ephesus write:
> These are the words of him who holds the seven stars in his right hand and walks among the seven golden lampstands: I know your deeds, your hard work and your perseverance. I know that you cannot tolerate wicked men, that you have tested those who claim to be apostles but are not, and have found them false. You have persevered and have endured hardships for my name, and have not grown weary.
> Yet I hold this against you: You have forsaken your first love. Remember the height from which you have fallen! Repent and do the things you did at first. If you do not repent, I will come to you and remove your lampstand from its place (Rev. 2:1-5).

What is fascinating about this passage is to compare Christ's words to the other churches in Revelation 2—3 with what He had to say to the church at Ephesus. For Smyrna, there was no warning. Instead, Christ spoke an affirmation to remain faithful in the midst of suffering and gave a stirring promise. For Pergamum, He spoke of a problem and gave a warning about it, but He also gave a promise. In Thyatira, Laodicea and Sardis, the pattern was the same. Philadelphia was like Smyrna—no warning given, only an affirmation and a promise.

What is my point? It is simply this: Ephesus was a great church. The Ephesians wouldn't put up with false doctrine. They were trying to change the moral climate of their world and had sacrificed to get to where they were. They sound a lot like the Evangelical Church in America today. However, once you compare Christ's words to Ephesus with those He spoke to the other churches, *you are struck by the fact that no promise was given to them!*

Even Laodicea received a promise from God. That fact would definitely have gotten the attention of the Ephesians. The promise listed in verse 7 is addressed to *all* the churches, not specifically to Ephesus. Jesus was saying loud and clear to the folks in Ephesus, "In the process of doing all the wonderful things you are doing, you have lost sight of the main thing. Repent and then go back to the things you did at first. Remember your passion for Me and your genuine concern for the lost and hurting in your world. Remember where you started; otherwise, I will come and remove your lampstand" (see Rev. 2:5).

Jesus is speaking of the inevitable sequence of events that takes place in any church that loses its heart for the lost. They lose a sense of Christ's special presence in their midst. Their ability to truly change their world begins to wither through the years. Every flock that declares its commitment to Christ bears a corporate responsibility. And we don't have to guess what it is, because a risen Christ made it absolutely clear:

> All authority in heaven and on earth has been given to me. Therefore go and make disciples of all nations, baptizing them in the name of the Father and of the Son and of the Holy Spirit, and teaching them to obey everything I have commanded you (Matt. 28:18-20).

In those final moments before Christ departed from the disciples, He said to them and to all who would follow in their footsteps, "If you forget everything else, if you don't do anything else, remember to do this one thing: Enable people who don't know of My love to come into a heartfelt relationship with Me. Then enable them to follow Me as disciples. *That is the bottom line. This has to be your first love*" (see Rev. 2:4).

The truth we must apply is the fact than an *organization* cannot make disciples. Even a *church* cannot make disciples. Disciples are birthed only by other disciples. If we have said yes to Christ, our responsibility is exactly the same as Peter's, James's and John's—to see that people come to faith in Christ, that they learn to follow Christ with all their heart and to help others do the same. It is every disciple's calling to help others come to such a passionate intimacy with Christ so that they too are inspired to reach out to others in need.

WHY WAS CHRIST SO INTENSE ABOUT DISCIPLESHIP?

Why was Christ so emphatic in His words to the disciples, the Ephesians and to us today?

The answer is simple: It is a struggle for all of us to keep our first love in focus. Let me use my church in Oregon as an example. Oregonians not only live in one of the most unchurched areas of the nation, but we also have the highest percentage of atheists in the United States according to a recent survey. Because of this fact, we are called to take atheists and turn them into flaming evangelists for Christ.[12] We're trying to take folks who believe in few, if any, absolutes—let alone the lordship of Christ—and call them to a holy life. We are calling them to a pure discipleship.

We are trying to take folks whose lifestyles and values run counter to God's Word and call them to submit to divine authority.

We are trying to convince them they should change the way they relate as husband and wife, the way they discipline their children, the way they spend their money and the way they use their time.

We are going to convince them to follow Christ so totally that they are probably going to end up rearranging their whole life. On top of that, they'll go out and hassle other folks with the same message!

This is *extremely hard work,* and it is precisely why Christ was so impassioned. It is easy to fall into the trap of having church for the already convinced. It is much easier to have worship and teaching times just for the believers. It is even easier to have a ministry that serves the community by feeding the poor and providing various community services. All of these efforts are important, but they are not the first priority. That is why it is so easy for the Church to get off track.

God Possesses Outrageous Love for Everyone

I fight to keep my priorities straight all the time. It takes a very determined effort on my part to establish relationships with folks outside of East Hill who don't know Christ. In fact, I can be so consumed with speaking, administration and counseling in any given week that I totally lose sight of what is really important in this whole process known as "church." When the Lord tries to get my attention back on His priorities—reaching out and discipling the lost—I find myself responding with comments like, "But, Lord, I am so busy. I am a pastor. I don't have time for real ministry!"

> *The most incredible news in all the cosmos is the fact that God is fervently seeking us.*

At a moment like that, I need to remind myself what discipleship is really about. God didn't create us because He needed someone to love. God definitely isn't lonely. He exists in relationship with God the Father, God the Son and God the Holy Spirit. At the very core of all reality, God exists in a perfect, loving relationship.

It is we who long for intimacy—an in-depth relationship. We were created in God's image—in the image of the Trinity. The most incredible news in all the cosmos is the fact that God is fervently seeking us. The sad truth is that many church folks don't even realize they can be part of this awesome romance. They don't understand just how passionate God is toward us. He calls us to a furious romance.

I think many believers tend to view God as a sort of Mr. Rogers, someone who gently sings over them as he takes off his shoes and puts on his sweater, somehow hoping the television broadcast will reach the lost.

No way! God is passionate about loving us. If we don't realize that fact, a pure-hearted discipleship will never make any sense to us, or, worse, it will be turned into a spiritual-growth program. *This is ultimately not about us. It's about God's furious love toward us.*

God Is Radical

I have discovered that God is radical about His love toward us. One incident really should have made me realize this: I remember watching 23mm antiaircraft shells flying toward my aircraft in the middle of the night. I had seen enough antiaircraft fire to know these tracers were going to hit me.

As I braced myself for the impact and coming catastrophe, I watched in amazement as the tracers suddenly veered off at a 90-degree angle. At that moment, I sensed the Lord whispering His love for me. Incidents like that get your attention!

Despite how this incident momentarily grabbed my attention, I later explained it away as simply an optical illusion. Sure, I had said yes to Christ several weeks before, but I planned to look Him up after I got out of Vietnam.

Several months later, as I flew against enemy positions near the border of North Vietnam and South Vietnam, I rolled in to attack some concealed antiaircraft guns the forward air controller had spotted. After only a few seconds in the attack run, numerous objects suddenly flashed by the aircraft. They were falling past me from above, not shooting up from the ground. As I pulled away from the target, the entire valley below erupted into a wall of explosions that I knew weren't caused by the few bombs I had dropped.

The forward air controller began screaming something incoherent over the radio. Once he finally calmed down, he told me I had just flown through an Arc Light raid. That meant B-52 bombers high overhead had dropped huge numbers of bombs into the same valley we had been attacking. We had been so low that we had not picked up their warnings broadcast over the radio. And for some reason, the forward air controller hadn't checked for Arc Light raids that day.

I had flown through a stack of bombs dropped from thousands of feet overhead. It is physically impossible for you to fly your plane through a stack of bombs. The Lord wasn't just whispering His love for me anymore. He was shouting in my ear!

God is radical about this love stuff! His heart for lost humanity will meet you in some really scary places. And if you choose to follow Him, you will end up in some equally scary places, which is the adventure, the romance and the soul-stirring experience of discipleship. I love Heinrich Arnold's definition of discipleship:

> Discipleship is not a question of our own doing; it is a matter of making room for God so that He can live in us.[13]

God Cares About Who We Are, Not What We Do

Over the last decade, I have read book after book regarding discipleship, only to find that many of them confuse *doing* with *being*. This is a tragic mistake, because the very thing Christ has called us to do—the thing that must remain our first love—is totally impossible to *do*. Therefore, the focus has to be on *being*.

You may say, "Wait a minute, Ted, you lost me with that last statement." Here is what I am talking about: Many people approach the challenge of discipleship by constructing a list of character traits they need to develop. They list various beliefs, practices and virtues they need to grow. Then a program is created to facilitate their progress.

I know most people mean well, but this relationship with God is about an *outrageous romance*. Their approach is like my making a checklist of what I need to do to be a good husband and then diligently checking off the duties one-by-one. When the final checkmark is made, I look at my wife and say, "There, I am a great husband now." That would be ridiculous.

The marriage relationship is about a romance! It is about a passionate partnership, not a checklist of character traits. Yes, it involves character—character birthed from the heart, from the depths of my soul. Sure, it involves acquiring certain skills. But romance has to come from the heart and not a man-made checklist.

> *Our relationship with Christ should mirror the marriage relationship—it is the greatest love story of all time.*

Marriage is the abandonment of my heart and soul in a risky experience of vulnerability and passion toward my wife. Our relationship with Christ should mirror the marriage relationship. God's love for us is the greatest love story of all time.

WHERE DO WE FIND CHRIST'S DISCIPLESHIP PRAYER FOR US?

Where can we find a concise description of what Christ is doing in our lives? Where can we find a cogent account of His discipleship plan for each of us? You don't have to look very far in the New Testament to find it. All you have to do is look at Christ's last prayer with His disciples in John 17.

He prayed specifically for you and me. Interestingly enough, of all the books I have read dealing with discipleship, I have not found one that used Christ's prayer as a pattern for discipleship, which is rather strange. Because if discipleship is primarily about *being* rather than *doing,* then this prayer is obviously where you should start.

In saying that the focus in discipleship has to be on Christ's work in you—*being* not just *doing*—I do not imply that this is a passive process. Being is always more challenging than just doing. The words of Christ's prayer for you will challenge you to the very core of your being if you read them carefully and reverently. A reverent response is appropriate when you come to John 17, as you listen to an extended conversation between God the Father and God the Son. It is a love dialogue of the Trinity.

The entire prayer covers three issues:

1. Christ's prayer for Himself—the shortest portion (vv. 1-5);
2. Christ's prayer for His disciples (vv. 6-19);
3. Christ's prayer for those who follow Him in the coming centuries (vv. 20-26).

I have created an expanded translation of Christ's prayer for you—the prayer He is praying for you right now. The author of Hebrews declares that Christ ever intercedes for us, and this is specifically what He is praying over you (see Heb. 7:24-25).

This is indeed a place where we should pull off our shoes and bow humbly before our God, knowing that He ever intercedes for us. This is Christ's discipleship prayer (based on John 17:13-23) for *you* today:

Now that I am coming back to You, Father, I am saying these things while I am still in the world's hearing so that [put your name here] *can know and experience My joy fully and completely and perfectly within.* [Joy]

I have given and communicated Your Word to [put your

name here] *and my other disciples. As a result, the world has hated them, because they haven't joined the world's way of thinking and living, just as I am not of the world.* [Holiness]

My prayer is not that You pull them out of the world, but that You protect and guard them from the evil one. They are not defined by this world, just as I am not defined by this world or a part of it. [Grace]

Make [put your name here] *holy, purify and heal and make* [put your name here] *and my other disciples wholly Yours by means of the truth. Your Word is the consecrating and healing truth.* [Truth]

In the same manner that You sent Me into the world—with a clear mission and purpose, I am sending [put your name here] *with the same mission and purpose. I have given Myself—consecrated Myself totally to that purpose and mission so that* [put your name here] *will be truth consecrated as well.* [Vision]

I am not just praying for those surrounding Me tonight, but also for those who will come to believe and trust in Me through their witness, so they would all be of one heart and one mind just as You, Father, are in Me and I in You. Then the world will believe that You did, indeed, send Me. I have given them the glory You gave to Me so that they would be one as We are one—I in them and You in Me. Then they will mature in this unity and oneness to the place that a lost world will recognize that You sent Me [Unity], *and that You love them as much as You love Me* [An Incredible Love].

This is Christ's discipleship plan for your life. This is Christ's methodology for reaching and redeeming a lost world. There are few passages in the entire Bible more important for us to understand as individuals and as the Church. This truly is holy ground! That is why we will spend the rest of this book coming to grips with Christ's discipleship plan found in John 17—His plan of healing discipleship and determined intimacy for our lives.

In the ensuing chapters, let me invite you to join with me in a journey of the heart and soul. We are going to be looking at six discipleship traits and how Christ develops them uniquely in our lives. And, finally, we will look at an evaluation of exactly where we presently are in this voyage of grace.

FINAL THOUGHTS

Let me once again emphasize as strongly as I can that discipleship ultimately is about Christ's outrageous love for us, *not* a plan or methodology. Read His prayer for you again and again, hopefully grasping as never before that this is about a divine romance—a call to pure discipleship, not a religious program.

I will never forget the first time I heard Mother Teresa interviewed on the evening news. The news anchor was obviously uncomfortable with being surrounded by so many dying and seriously ill people, but little Mother Teresa beamed from ear to ear as she tended to the desperately sick.

Throughout the interview she was in constant motion, caring for others. The more she responded in simple but profound statements to the questions posed by the reporter, the more my eyes filled with tears. She was talking about the Jesus I first started following years ago in a bunker in Vietnam. She was talking about my first love—the Lover of my soul.

Through the years, having been in four different denominations, I have seen so much church "junk" and denominational politics. When I read several of Mother Teresa's books, her words were like water, cleansing my soul from all the religious crud

I had waded through. I openly wept as she described her daily routine:

> Jesus feeds us with His love; He becomes our spiritual nourishment in the Eucharist, and we feed Him with compassion in the disguise of the distress of the poor.[14]

What a graphic picture of a pure discipleship! What a glorious description of the divine romance Christ wants to bring us into!

Early in the morning, frequently before the rising of the sun, the sisters working with Mother Teresa gather for worship and communion together. Out of that encounter with the goodness of God, they give to others. In the process, they discover the needy are actually Jesus in disguise, giving back to them. They find themselves involved in this incredible, life-transforming love adventure known as being discipled by Christ. Please don't misunderstand—Mother Teresa would never have presented her relationship with Christ as a constant experience of effortless delight. She cut away any fluffy idealism with her statement about the demands Christ put on her life:

> Jesus can demand a great deal from us. It is precisely in those instances when He demands a great deal from us that we should give Him a beautiful smile.[15]

Come with me to the high country of Christ's call to a pure discipleship. I guarantee this will put a lasting smile on your face like nothing else.

CHAPTER TWO

HIGH FLIGHT

*How to Gauge Your Journey as
a Disciple of Christ*

A flight surgeon who was my passenger was required to fly in an operation aircraft a few hours a month. I had been given the task of taking him along on a rather crammed flight schedule. As a maintenance test pilot, I needed to perform postmaintenance tests on the engine as well as oversee a group of students during a formation training flight, which would be taking off behind us. I didn't have a minute to spare, so it was critical to reach altitude as soon as possible.

I decided not to wait until I was at altitude to test the maximum performance capabilities of the new engine. Instead, I executed a maximum performance takeoff. I asked the flight surgeon if he became airsick easily. I wanted to know if he could deal with blasting off the end of the runway with everything to the wall.

Carrying himself as if he knew what he was talking about, he responded, "I never get airsick!" With my best *Top Gun* smile, I said, "Hang on. I feel the need for speed."

Of course, the start-up was a total disaster, which is normal when you're in a hurry. Part of the radar transponder equipment went out in the front cockpit, but there was a backup in the rear seat. I talked the flight surgeon through what I needed him to do to operate the equipment. I could tell he was struggling to understand me; he had his head down as he frantically searched for the right switch. Finally, he managed to get the right code setting just as we got clearance for takeoff, and I pulled out on the runway.

I hammered the throttle home, and we ripped down the runway with everything to the wall. I snapped up the landing gear, keeping the plane as low as I could. When we came to the end of the runway, I pulled the plane into the vertical. With the engine working perfectly, we blasted straight up, right out of sight.

That is when the flight surgeon lost it—big time! I had to turn off the intercom. It became apparent that he was checking out his stomach lining. He was experiencing what is politely called motion sickness.

Upon landing, I discovered why he'd had such a rough time. We had been so rushed in the start-up and taxi process that he didn't have time to adjust his seat. Apparently, an unusually tall flight student had been in the aircraft prior to him, so the seat was to the floor. When I hammered the throttle forward, the flight surgeon found himself sitting down in a hole, smashed against the seat. Once I pulled us up into the vertical, the instrument panel towered over him, the outside world passed by in a blur, and the horizon was nowhere in sight.

If you ever have been at sea on a rough day, you know that to avoid becoming seasick, you focus on the horizon instead of your immediate surroundings. This is also true when it comes to flying in high-performance aircraft. The poor flight surgeon could have enjoyed the flight if he had been able to get his head out of the cockpit.

Discipleship—as God created it to be—is a head-out-of-the-cockpit, rip-roaring experience of the heart. Yet, sadly, today we frequently present it as a head-down, learn-the-doctrine, watch-the-instruments head-trip. It is perceived as an ordered, grinding, skill-acquisition, character-building experience.

> *Discipleship—as God created it to be—is a head-out-of-the-cockpit, rip-roaring experience of the heart.*

Sure, discipline is involved. That is why it is called discipl[in]eship—discipline is at the root of discipleship. Flying a high-performance plane requires discipline in preparation, but ultimately it is not only about discipline and rote skills. Instead, a great pilot *feels* the plane. There is a sense of living on the edge, an understanding that you are dealing with something so powerful that it demands respect. Above all, in these moments of risk, challenge and discipline, *you are fully and radically alive!*

EXPERIENCING THE UNIQUE PASSION OF DISCIPLESHIP

C. S. Lewis summed up our situation clearly and compellingly, "Our Lord finds our desires, not too strong, but too weak. We are halfhearted creatures, fooling about with drink, sex, and ambition, when infinite joy is offered to us."[1]

I remember when I first read that statement; it struck my heart with incredible force. I was an alcoholic, sex addict, rage-oholic and an arrogant, ambitious fighter pilot. Mr. Lewis had just articulated the role I had assumed. But I had recently said yes to Christ, and I wanted to know about this infinite joy Mr. Lewis spoke of. In the years ahead, I slowly discovered that Christ didn't have a job description but a passion for me.

Christ's prayer in John 17 tells us loud and clear that discipleship is ultimately about God's passion for us. Sadly, so many believers think the Great Commission in Matthew 28 is a job description. If you stop and think about it, that perspective is absurd. You can't fulfill the Great Commission by *doing*. It only can be fulfilled by the right kind of *being*. Discipleship is making room for God in our lives so that He can passionately live *in* us and *with* us.

It is difficult for any of us to believe or even remotely understand how passionate Christ is toward each of us—personally. I love the parable the Danish philosopher Kierkegaard used to tell to illustrate His passionate love for each of us. Let me put this story in my own words:

Suppose there was a king or mighty ruler who loved a humble, simple young woman who lived in the ghetto. This ruler was like no other. Every statesman, every member of the United Nations and even every drug lord on the streets of the ghetto where this young lady lived trembled before his power.

No one could stand in his presence.

No one could match his power.

Yet his heart melted with love for this poverty-stricken young lady.

The king struggled with how he could express his love for her. If he ordered her brought to his estate and showered her with expensive gifts, cars and clothing, surely she would not resist. In fact, no one would dare resist him. But because she wouldn't resist him, would that mean she loved him? Would she honestly want to be at his side?

If he showed up in her part of town with a stretch limo, bodyguards and the symbols and substance of power, wealth and glory, wouldn't that overwhelm her as well?

The ruler didn't want a fawning servant. He wanted a lover. He wanted to share his love over the gulf that lay between them. And in the process, his love would transform an unequal into royalty. There was only one option—the ruler came as a common worker and set aside his privilege and power in order to win her hand.

Discipleship means making room for that lover and ruler in our life. Any other definition gets our head down in the cockpit, smashed against our circumstances, watching life pass by in a blur. It is only a matter of time before we get sick of the whole thing.

George Barna made an interesting observation about folks who are born again:

> The fact that a substantial slice of the adult, born-again population could walk away from church without any indication of returning ought to make us pause and reflect.[2]

Barna didn't go on to identify that one of the reasons folks bail on church is the lack of understanding of biblical discipleship, yet he did point out the major reason for the mass exodus—individuals don't feel the Church is relevant. That lack of relevancy is powerfully answered once we realize the passion and purpose of discipleship. The joy experienced addresses the deepest issues of our hearts.

EVALUATING THE PASSIONATE COUPLETS OF DISCIPLESHIP IN OUR LIFE

Speaking about what affects the deepest issues of our hearts brings us back to Christ's prayer in John 17. In Christ's final prayer prior to the Cross, we hear His heart not only for the disciples who surrounded Him in the Upper Room that fateful night but also for those who would follow Him down through the ages to the end of time.

If you read and reread Christ's prayer, you begin to realize that it is a magnificent series of three couplets. By couplets, I mean truths that are held in dynamic tension—truths that seem to be almost mutually exclusive but to Christ, they are not. His prayer profoundly portrays the genius of the "and." Discipleship is about both joy *and* holiness, grace *and* truth, vision *and* unity—all embedded in an incredible love.

In the Christian community, an uneasy tension definitely exists between joy and holiness. If people are only bubbles and joy all the time, without any sense of holiness in their lives, they end up being spiritual space cadets! On the other hand, if they are totally into holiness and view with suspicion any explosive expressions of joy, they end up becoming self-righteous, uptight, religious hardheads!

All six of these discipleship aspects—joy, holiness, grace, truth, vision, and unity—are in dynamic relationship. Grace has to *influence* our concept of holiness, or we easily slide into the spiritual abuse of others. Additionally, grace lies at the very heart of joy. Further, God's truth has to influence our vision or we become deluded; biblical truth must influence our sense of unity, or we settle for a unity of emotion and preference or political correctness.

Every one of these "being" truths is dynamically related to the other. Therefore, balance and sensitivity are critically important to these truths. In fact, our growth as passionate-hearted disciples of Christ can be evaluated in light of our increasing sense of balance and sensitivity as they relate to these six being truths in our life.

At the end of each of the remaining chapters, specific questions and statements about each discipleship trait will be available for you to answer in a miniquiz format. Once you have calculated all the scores for each trait, you will enter them into the final overall diagram in chapter 12. After you have calculated your scores and read chapter 12, you will know where you are in the discipleship process.

Discipleship is indeed the marvelous, romantic adventure of following passionately after Christ; however, our growth in that relationship can be observed and evaluated at the same time. It is not a totally mystical experience. Like a great marriage, the relationship and love deepen as the sensitivity and balance increase. Yet the recklessness and creativity are still present in this whole adventure we call discipleship. The best analogy that comes to my mind is found in my all-time favorite poem about flying, written by John Gillespie Magee, Jr.

High Flight

Oh! I have slipped the surly bonds of earth
And danced the skies of laughter-silvered wings;

Sunward I've climbed, and joined the tumbling
   mirth
Of sun-split clouds—and done a hundred things
   You have not dreamed of—
   wheeled and soared and swung
High in the sunlit silence.
   Hov'ring there,
I've chased the shouting wind along, and flung
My eager craft through footless halls of air.
Up, up the long, delirious burning blue
I've topped the windswept heights with easy grace
   Where never lark, or even eagle flew—
And, while with silent lifting mind I've trod
   The high untrespassed sanctity of space,
Put out my hand, and touched the face of God.[3]

You might be saying, "Ted, you turn everything into a flying story." But stick with me; take a look at the picture on the next page. This is a superb illustration of the dynamic relationships among the truths that are so foundational to discipleship. You can sense the tension between each pair of couplets as the airplane attempts to find its balance by using all six traits.

Notice that an effective airplane can respond in all three axes—the propeller powering higher or lower, the elevator changing the altitude and the ailerons imparting rolling motion. Referring back to the dynamic tension of the six discipleship traits, can you see how the traits are in pairs, and how each pair resembles one of the three axes? Joy and holiness help change your movement in the Spirit; therefore, they resemble the airplane's elevator. Grace and truth power you to flight in the Spirit; therefore, they resemble the propeller. Vision and unity help you stay on course; therefore, they are extensions of the wings.

Additionally, there is a dynamic relationship between the two extremes in each axis. In other words, you can go up, but you also can go down. One without the other is disastrous! For example, grace without truth is disastrous when you soar on the winds of the Holy Spirit. However, as the pilot gains more skill and sensitivity to the aircraft and maintains balance, he or she is able to experience great freedom.

Also notice that there are two folks in the biplane. The truths of discipleship are never learned by sitting in a classroom listening to some sermon or lecture. These truths are relational and are learned primarily in the struggles and victories of daily life. That is the way Jesus taught the disciples—very little lecture and lots of personal experience.

You have seen me cast out demons, heal the sick and raise the dead, now it is your turn (see Matt. 10:1-10).

And Jesus didn't say that just to the Twelve. He gave that challenge to many others (see Luke 10:1-17). Interestingly enough, when He called people into the dynamics of discipleship, He always sent them out *two* by *two*.

GETTING THIS THING AIRBORNE

Let's get this thing airborne! I absolutely love the first thing that Christ prays for us: He wants us to know and experience *His* joy.

I remember the first discipleship program I got involved in after I said yes to Christ. I was told that discipleship is about understanding correct doctrine, and Christ calls you to be His disciple. Well, I sure loved Christ, so I gave it a shot. But it didn't take long before I felt like I was chewing on wood chips—spiritually. I was memorizing Scripture, lots of it, and that was good. I was learning tons of theological truth, and that was good. But something inside was rapidly draining from my life—joy—the joy that I had when I first started following Christ. The program felt like I was learning how to write love letters, but there wasn't anyone I was madly in love with. It was like being perpetually stuck in ground school, never being allowed to experience the thrill, adventure and risk of soaring in the Spirit on laughter-silvered wings.

Do you remember the joy you had when you first came to know Christ? The thrill of everything being new, the joy of God's being so near and His presence being so real?

Why is it that so many Christians lose their sense of joy along the way? What is strange is that Christ's prayer makes it clear that the joy He is speaking about is totally secure—it is *His* joy (see John 17:13). But that is the problem, isn't it? We keep forgetting it is *His* joy we are talking about. It is not based on circumstance or how we happen to feel. It is not even based on our depth of correct understanding of theological truth.

> *Do you remember the joy you had when you first came to know Christ?*

Please don't misunderstand me. I am not saying theological truth isn't important, because it is. However, there is something even deeper at work here. It is a joy based on *His presence* in our lives.

I vividly remember a very difficult time in my life when it seemed that everything had turned into a cacophony of discontent. I hung in there, but my fingernails got rather fatigued. I told myself theological truth every day, quoting the promises of God. I deeply believed them, but the pit only seemed to get deeper.

I prayed in the Holy Spirit (see Jude 24) day and night to build myself up, because this situation was destroying me. Yet it seemed the bulldozers of hell were tearing me apart. Then I sensed Christ saying to me, *I didn't ask you to have joy in times like these, but to have* My *joy."*

Jesus wasn't playing a word game with me. Instead, He was calling me into a deeper romance of the soul. He was bidding me to come and not try to be the strong one in the relationship, which is tough for an ex-marine fighter pilot, but instead to fall into His arms. He was calling me to abandon my life to Him to a whole new depth, to trust Him even if I never got out of that pit. But being in a pit with Christ—in His presence—is better than being in any palace you could ever imagine. You see, for a pure-hearted disciple of Christ, joy is a given because it is His joy. We all have huge problems at some time in our life; we can get our head shoved down in life and become deeply disoriented. Yet it is when we seek and recognize Christ's joy and to find the balance act in each couplet of traits that we learn to fly on the wings of God's grace. Let's find out how that's done!

Joy

Holiness

CHAPTER THREE

THE KILLJOYS

Finding and Eliminating the Killers of Christ's Joy

Now that I am coming back to You, Father, I am saying these things while I am still in the world's hearing so that [put your name here] *can know and experience My joy fully and completely and perfectly within.*
(SEE JOHN 17:13.)

In Christ's prayer for us, He declares we can experience His joy, which is an incredible promise of security. If our joy is so secure, if it is based on Christ's presence in our lives, then why is it such a common experience for us as believers to have the initial joy of following Christ leak right out of our lives? Because there are some major killjoys that damage our relationship with the lover of our soul—things that get our head and heart down and totally disorient us.

Paul, one of the few in the New Testament to do so, exposes the struggles of his soul to the reader. In Philippians, Paul is in prison. His efforts are under constant attack by rivals. He has spent 20-plus grueling years traveling from town to town sharing the gospel. And what are the results of his efforts? Many people have deserted him, and he doesn't have much to show for his sweat and tears. Yet Philippians is one of Paul's most joy-filled letters:

> Finally, my brothers, rejoice in the Lord! It is no trouble for me to write the same things to you again, and it is a safeguard for you. Watch out for those dogs, those men who do evil, those mutilators of the flesh. For it is we who are the circumcision, we who worship by the Spirit of God, who glory in Christ Jesus, and who put no confidence in the flesh—though I myself have reasons for such confidence.
>
> But whatever was to my profit I now consider loss for the sake of Christ. What is more, I consider everything a loss compared to the surpassing greatness of knowing Christ Jesus my Lord, for whose sake I have lost all things. I consider them rubbish, that I may gain Christ and be found in him, not having a righteousness of my own that comes from the law, but that which is through faith in Christ—the righteousness that comes from God and is by faith. I want to know Christ and the power of his resurrection and the fellowship of sharing in his sufferings, becoming like him in his death (vv. 3:1-4,7-10).

This passage has to be the greatest personal response to Christ's prayer in John 17 found in the entire Bible. I can never read the passage without my heart pounding a little faster. That is the kind of passion with which I want to live life. That is the kind of abandonment with which I want to follow Christ. That is the kind of pure-hearted *disciple* I want to become.

I am sure it is true for you as well. Otherwise, you wouldn't be reading this book. However, such a transformation will never take place in your life or mine until we learn how to effectively deal with the great killers of Christ's joy in our lives.

> *If our joy is so secure, if it is based on Christ's presence in our lives, then why is it such a common experience to have the initial joy of following Christ leak right out of our lives?*

A KILLER RELIGION

The first killjoy we have to deal with is a killer religion. There is nothing that destroys the joy Christ has for us like abusive religion. I have seen more zealous new believers destroyed by legalism and abusive religion than by anything else for this simple reason: When the zeal level is sky high, legalism loves to sneak in the back door and destroy everything in sight in the name of God.

Paul is emphatic about his disdain for abusive religion. He refers to the promoters of such a relationship with God as "dogs" (Phil. 3:2, *THE MESSAGE*). Now he wasn't calling them house pets. In Paul's time, dogs were infrequently used as house pets. Instead, they were vicious scavengers that usually traveled in packs. Today, we might say, "They are like a pack of wolves."

It Is Abusive

Abusive religion and legalism are about substituting rules, rituals and regulations—usually in a subtle way—for an intimate relationship with Christ. Over a period of time, the focus shifts from what God has done for us to what we can do for God.

Abusive religion loves to make disciples. In fact, it goes out of its way to systematically train and control through shame and guilt. That is why legalism tends to run in families and entire churches. It is one of the toughest generational curses to break, because the individual has been so thoroughly programmed. The symptoms of spiritual abuse can closely parallel those of sexual abuse, which is why it can be so difficult to help the person become accustomed to healthy, intimate relations with the Lord. Grace, forgiveness, freedom and joy can feel strange to the individual—almost unhealthy.

It Is Demanding

When you first came to Christ, you were joyous because you simply loved Christ. You were delighted over what He had done for you, and you didn't know *all the rules* yet! Then someone came along and said something like, "Well, that is great that you have decided to follow Christ. But if you want to move into the deeper life or become a spirit-filled believer or get really sanctified or _____ (fill in the blank), then you . . ." and out came the list of what you needed to do to become that someone's definition of a mature believer. It is common for the list to go all the way to the floor. What makes this totally crazy is that after you hang around church life for a while, you will discover that the lists are not consistent—especially the "being a disciple" list.

The killer is there is no way you can meet the list of demands. If the truth be known, the individual harassing you isn't fulfilling the list him- or herself. The individual is just operating a religious pyramid scheme, and you end up carrying the load.

Romance Is Key

Once you put your neck into the noose of abusive religion, you end up concerned with how you look, perform and come across, eventually focusing solely on your own insecurities instead of the romance of walking with Christ.

"But, Ted, that's nuts. Why would anyone ever settle for such a destructive option?" you might ask.

The keyword is "romance" in any healthy discipleship relationship with Christ.

The keyword is "romance." It is the keyword in any healthy discipleship relationship with Christ. But it is also the word that terrifies so many in our culture today. For the last 20-plus years, I have counseled folks who struggle with one of the reasons for this fear—sexual bondage. Our church has such an extensive ministry in this area that secular agencies are beginning to refer individuals to our ministry for help. The church can become a healing center in the community—what a concept!

You only have to listen for a couple of years to folks struggling with sexual bondage to begin to realize several things. First, the Church in America is filled with this problem. When I speak at a large men's gathering, it is not unusual for 70 to 80 percent of the men present to come forward seeking help in this area of their lives.

That response shouldn't surprise anyone, because the rates for drug addiction, divorce and domestic violence in the Church are no different from those for society at large. And I'm sad to say, so much of the Church has become involved in a performance orientation that there is little help for those who struggle other than to hear someone preach against whatever it is they are doing.

Many addicts are very social creatures. They hide the vulnerable part of their life. No one gets the whole picture, not even their mate. They do not know much about themselves, in part because of their sense of unworthiness, despite their excellent outward performance at times. Deep within they feel defective. They are uncomfortable being in their own presence. They don't know how to handle their emotions and, in fact, struggle to understand their feelings. This struggle eventually leads to their living a depleted and exhausted life.

Simply put, romance, real romance, is a foreign concept to them, one they desperately need to experience with their Lord and Savior. But because of their wounds and struggles, abusive, religious legalism seems to make more sense to them. The barking dogs of performance and personal pain are a familiar sound they have learned to follow.

There are three clear indications that people have been bitten by the dogs of abusive religion. These symptoms are not so much learned in the church as they are learned in the home and then practiced in the church.

1. They have a very difficult time with grace—resting is difficult. They will find ways to push away God's grace or to refuse gifts from other people. They end up going without.

When I first started attending church, I noticed something rather strange. I hadn't grown up in the Church, so I found the behavior bizarre at times. Someone would sing a song, share a word or play some music during the service; and if you told the person he or she did a great job, the person would have the weirdest response, "Oh, it wasn't me. It was the Lord." I would walk away thinking, *It sure looked like that person was up there singing.* In the name of humility, the individual was killing him- or herself. Through the years I noticed the more intense that kind of behavior became, the more people sought affirmation and approval in hidden and even destructive ways. It was one strange system!

Addicts frequently live like that. Addiction is inflamed by deprivation, overextension, denial and repressed feelings. All of this leads to an ever-deeper sense of depletion. That is why legalism is so deadly. You work harder and harder for an ever-fading reward.

There is no way to win in this system. You either walk away from God angered that He would so abuse you, or you just keep on going, waiting for the sweet by-and-by when you will get your reward. You also may drive yourself to keep up the appearance of having made it, which can make you uncompassionate toward others. You miss the outrageous joy of walking with Christ in a romantic adventure that starts *now* and extends throughout *eternity*. Is that what you had in mind?

2. They can understandably have a difficult time relating to spiritual authority—trusting is challenging. Those who have experienced the misuse of power—which is what legalism and abusive religion are ultimately about—will find ways to defend themselves from being abused again. They can react either in open defiance or unquestioning compliance when faced with authority figures. Either option is a tragic reaction. Scripture frequently relates our spiritual growth to a healthy response to authority (see Eph. 4:11-13; Heb. 13:17; Jas. 4:7; 1 Pet. 2:13-14).

3. They can struggle and become confused with issues concerning personal responsibility boundaries. They may constantly procrastinate because of their past performance systems. They were taught performance equaled value, so they put off the inevitable evaluation. They were taught in their family, by experience, that no amount of performance would result in the promised prize of love, acceptance or recognition. Therefore, deep within, they knew they again were going to be disappointed.

Or they may be caught in the other extreme of staying on the treadmill of incessant *doing*. They are frequently a hyperresponsible burden bearer. It is nearly impossible for them to say no to other people's requests and problems. They may find themselves getting angry at times but inevitably repent, because, after all, a good Christian never says no to any request for help. Of course, they forget that Jesus did say no:

- At the death of Lazarus (see John 11:4).
- At the request of Peter not to talk about the Cross; in fact, Jesus openly rebuked him for his comment (see Matt. 16:23).
- At the temple gate "Beautiful," where the crippled man sat (Jesus must have walked past the crippled man many times without responding to his requests for help) (see Acts 3:1-10).

Hyperresponsible Christians have been so hammered by a performance orientation that they keep on getting up to try harder the next time, which is why at some point they end up feeling numb and dry inside. They have never tasted the delicious waters of pure grace.

Grace and Joy Overflow from the Same Source

It is interesting that the terms "joy" and "grace" come from the same root word in the New Testament. Grace means that I don't have to earn God's love, approval or smile. God is always smiling at me, which is the source of my joy.

No wonder the two words are related!

In fact, I can't stop God's smiling at me, because I didn't make Him start smiling in the *first place*. We keep forgetting that whether we serve Him or not, God will not love us any more or less.

What I receive from serving in His name is the joy of partnering with Him and rewards in heaven (see Matt. 16:27). I think the reward will be the joy of watching video replays of how God worked through our lives as we trusted in Him, which will lead to eternal joy—the joy of seeing other lives touched and changed by God's grace working through us. If we miss the delicious waters of God's grace flowing through us to others, we end up in the reeking swamp of cynicism. Nothing is sadder than a cynical believer.

A KILLER BALANCE SHEET

The second spiritual killjoy is a killer balance sheet. It is critical that we as passionate-hearted disciples carefully evaluate our activities. It is critical for us to do that, because many people are looking for joy in all the wrong places. Paul declared, "Whatever was to my profit I now consider loss" (Phil. 3:7). That was Paul's balance sheet—his profit and loss statement.

There are things in my life that, like Paul, I used to look on with much pride. Now I consider them of little value. Paul's words in this passage are strong; he is passionately making his point. The actual word he uses, *skubala*, which has been translated "rubbish" or "garbage," isn't quite so polite a term. It is related to the concept of cow pies for those of you with a farming background. He is basically saying, "It ain't worth it."

What'll It Be?

Life consists of a series of tradeoffs, for the simple reason that you can't live for two things at the same time. I have discovered that the things I gave up to follow Christ —which I thought were so important at the time—not only were unimportant but also completely destructive. I just couldn't see it at the time.

Of course, I have to admit that for a period of time I thought I had sacrificed big time for Christ by walking away from flying to respond to His call in my life. Those thoughts ended the day I watched the movie *The Great Santini*. It is the story of a Marine Corps fighter pilot—I was immediately sucked in. I soon began to realize I wasn't watching a movie; instead, I was watching a replay of what my life would have been *if I hadn't responded to Christ's challenge*.

The movie was a prophetic picture of where I had been headed and why Christ so emphatically told me to walk away from military flying as a career. It wasn't my ultimate calling.

I sat on the couch with tears streaming down my face. I was crying from the depths of my soul as I watched this man destroy his son, his marriage and his family—nearly everything near and dear to him. What was worse, he couldn't even see it.

Oh, sure, he played the hero at the end of the movie, going down with his plane so that it didn't crash in a populated area. After the funeral, as the family drove down the highway, you could tell they were somewhat relieved they would no longer have to put up with an abusive dad and husband.

I sat there repenting and weeping for joy all at the same time. I repented for having thought I had given up so much to follow Christ, yet I was filled with joy for the change God had brought into my life.

Are You Ready to Let Go?

It is important that I be totally honest at this point: Being a passionate-hearted disciple *will* require you to give up everything. Initially, it doesn't feel that great. But down the road, once you have placed everything in Christ's hands—given up everything—you suddenly realize you never had it so good!

God didn't send me to pastor a conservative, cargo plane of a church. He called me to a fighter-pilot place known as East Hill Church, where we constantly push the limits and are committed to seriously hurting hell.

> *Being a passionate-hearted disciple* will *require you to give up everything. But down the road, once you have placed everything in Christ's hands—you suddenly realize you never had it so good!*

Frequently, we can end up lacking Christ's joy in our lives because we are holding on to things we know we need to yield to Him. The joy isn't there because we have totally missed the joy of the divine exchange and transformation that takes place when we finally let go.

Got anything you are struggling with giving up? Go ahead, risk it all in Him. I double-dog dare you. You will never regret the decision.

A MISPLACED AMBITION

The final killjoy is a misplaced ambition that eventually ends up killing the joy within. I love the *Amplified* translation of the first part of Philippians 3:10:

> [For my determined purpose is] that I may know Him [that I may progressively become more deeply and intimately acquainted with Him . . .].

It is interesting that Paul doesn't say his number one ambition is to start churches, get rewards in heaven or even win people to Christ. His number one ambition is to develop an ever-deepening, intimate relationship with Christ. What is really amazing about that statement is the fact that Paul made that declaration near the end of his life. Intimacy with Christ truly was Paul's life ambition.

Whoop It Up

Being a pure-hearted disciple is really about learning how to grow in intimacy with another—the Savior of your soul. As in any deepening relationship, you can't just coast. You need to *whoop it up*!

It takes time to know someone, and that includes Christ. I know Jesus a lot better now than I did five years ago, for the simple reason that I have spent *fun* time with Him alone—not going to Him just with my sorrow but with my *joy*. You can't develop a relationship with anyone in a crowd.

For example, I try to spend some fun time with Christ each day. Once I started making that a goal in my life, praying stopped being such a difficult spiritual exercise. My prayers have become less flowery and spiritual sounding. I am learning to talk to Christ on a continuous basis. If my sole ambition in life is to know Him, I want to know His thoughts and ideas on everything!

I love doing triathlons, so I spend a fair amount of time in physical training throughout the year. It is a great time to talk to the Lord. When I am running, I find myself asking questions like, "Lord, how can I develop a better stride?" or "Lord, why did you give me such wide feet? They look like swim fins when I am running." On the saddle, I may ask, "Lord, is there a better way to climb this hill on the bike?" or in the pool, "Lord, why is swimming a survival sport for me?"

You may think, *Come on, Ted, is God interested in your asking Him how to run or bike?* Well, He is, if you want to keep your joy. You might ask, "What do you mean?"

If you want to lose your joy in life, then talk to God *only* about the heavy or spiritual issues. Folks who talk to God only about serious spiritual issues usually end up looking like candidates for an acid indigestion commercial.

Whooping it up is more than just continually talking to God. Through the years, my wife, Diane, and I have worked hard at having a talk a day, a date a week and a getaway to whoop it up at least every three months. I have discovered this plan also works well for deepening my relationship with the Lord.

It is critical that I begin to see my relations with the Lord within a romantic framework. My understanding of discipleship is totally transformed if I come to see it as a process of growing in intimacy with the lover of my soul instead of a disciplined program in doing the right thing.

If, when spending time with my wife, I merely focus on doing the right thing but don't respond from my soul out of my love for her, our relationship would soon die from the inside out. *Sadly, that is exactly what has happened to so many of Christ's followers as they have tried to walk in discipleship.*

Keep It Up

After you whoop it up, you need to *keep it up*, because it is one thing to love each other in a marriage but another thing entirely to truly *like* each other through the years.

Diane and I recently had one of those Mount Saint Helen disagreements. We are not like those pastoral couples you might see on Christian TV, always smiling—you know, the perfect couple. We are not like that; *we have a marriage just like yours!*

A few minutes after the disagreement ended, we made up and were doing fine. After we both had apologized and reaffirmed our love for each other, I found myself asking the questions, *How did we come through that so well? Because we've been doing it for 30-plus years?*

Only one answer is possible: Because we have decided to be friends—warts and all. Sometimes our warts rub against one another. But things really get interesting when we realize that *God doesn't have any warts.* Therefore, when conflicts arise in our relationship with Him, we feel threatened. Why? Because we instinctively know who is going to have to change big-time—us!

You can hear this discomfort in Christian circles all the time. I remember a little chorus that was popular a number of years ago: I am so glad that Jesus loves me . . . Jesus loves even me.

The chorus seems to imply that Jesus loves lots of folks, but loving *you*, that's a real stretch. That is a total lie. Jesus doesn't "even" love you, He *so* loves you with all of your warts (see John 3:16).

True discipleship—becoming a passionate-hearted disciple and walking through this short journey we call life with a determined intimacy with God—is *never possible until you begin to catch a glimpse of God's outrageous love for* you. When you do, a supernatural joy, a reach-out-and-touch-the-face-of-God joy, is unleashed in your life!

Trust It Up

Finally, we need to *trust it up*. There is a question that thinking readers of Scripture have to ask themselves about the life of David: *How could anyone so flawed finish life with the reputation of being a man after God's own heart, which is God's own evaluation of the man?* (see Acts 13:22).

Scripture has more to say about David's life than anyone outside of Christ. I think that is because his life is such a classic example of a disciple of the heart. Two scenes from his life stand out with unique brilliance.

Scene one. David is bringing the Ark of the Covenant into Jerusalem and is whooping it up. He is bursting with joy over the fact that God's manifest presence is coming to His people. He starts cartwheeling down the street, or doing the funky chicken, in front of the Ark of the Covenant. His wife, however, is scandalized and doesn't mind telling David of her displeasure. David responds by saying, "I will rejoice and celebrate my God. I don't care how I look, because this isn't about me, it is about my passion for Him" (see 2 Sam. 6:21-22).

Scene two. David gets his head down in the cockpit of life. He gets totally disoriented. He finds himself being declared a great warrior, king, statesman and poet. He has accomplished all of this by his 30s or 40s. He has reached the pinnacle of power, and he has achieved everything. That is why he finds himself walking around a rooftop watching a woman take a bath and *going middle-aged crazy*! Fortunately, a friend, Nathan, confronted him before his soul teetered over the cliff of total destruction. How could a servant confront a king? And how would the king respond?

After watching one president lie and authorize hush money to cover up his crimes; after watching another president solemnly lie to an entire nation, declaring that he did not have an extramarital affair; after watching both "kings"—presidents—deny the dark facts of their lives, it is amazing to read David's response:

I have sinned against the LORD (2 Sam. 12:13).

David danced before an audience of one, so he repented before an audience of one. David's single-heartedness typified his life. Whether cartwheeling in front of the manifest presence of God or lying prostrate on the ground broken before God, David's heart was always set in one place—passionate pursuit of the Lord. He always *trusted up* in life. He was a passionate-hearted disciple all the days of his life, which eventually led to a purity of heart.

THE ROAD BACK HOME

Repenting of his sins, David turned back to his true course in life. He always managed to get his head out of the cockpit of self-orientation, look up and behold the greatness and grace of God. David was able to walk in the supernatural joy of God's love for him all the days of his life. Is walking burden free, completely engulfed in God's joy-filled presence, calling out to you? God wants you to come home.

How are you doing at *being* a passionate-hearted disciple of Christ? Let's start by finding out more about how you relate to Christ as His disciple and how you approach issues related to having a joy-filled heart. Read each question or statement and circle the number that best corresponds to your answer.

1. Do you have a hard time relaxing?

Most of the time		Sometimes		Not at all
1	2	3	4	5

2. Do you have trouble trusting and relating to spiritual authority?

Most of the time		Sometimes		Not at all
1	2	3	4	5

3. Do you have a hard time *not* overextending yourself? Is it a challenge for you to say no?

Most of the time		Sometimes		Not at all
1	2	3	4	5

4. I have given up a lot to follow the Lord. Do you struggle with that thought?

Most of the time		Sometimes		Not at all
1	2	3	4	5

5. Is it difficult for you to find time to pray?

Most of the time		Sometimes		Not at all
1	2	3	4	5

Score _____ (Add together the numbers you circled.)

This score will be added to the results from chapter 4 and the total score for Joy will be entered in the appropriate space on the Discipleship Development Analysis in chapter 12.

CHAPTER FOUR

OF GNATS AND NUCLEARS

God Is Opening the Door—Will You Enter In?

*Now that I am coming back to You, Father, I am saying these things
while I am still in the world's hearing so that* [put your name here] *can
know and experience My joy fully and completely and perfectly within.*
(*SEE JOHN 17:13.*)

Many people say that love and romance make the world go
round. And if all the love songs are correct, they might be right.
However, we can have a real problem with romance when it
comes to God, because we don't understand the joy factor. Say
we overheard the following conversation of a couple supposedly
madly in love with one another.

He says, "You know dear, I am really looking forward to our wedding day. I'm really in love with you, and I wish we could spend more time together. There is a greater depth of joy and passion we have yet to experience!"

She says, "You are right. In fact, I think I will read another book that talks about the potential of the relationship we could have. I'm sure that will really bless me."

Not to be deterred, he passionately replies, "Well, I'm glad you are reading and studying about the relationship we could have, but I want to hold you close and share my heart with you. You are the joy of my life!"

To which she analytically responds, "Yes, intimacy is important; in fact, it is a lovely word. I have studied the Greek and Hebrew meanings of the term and find them fascinating. Let me give you this research paper I have written to summarize my findings."

Our response would obviously be "Say what?" That is one stiff woman! The fellow ought to drop her as quickly as he can and get a girl who is still breathing. This woman will bring little joy to his life. *Yet frequently that is the way we live out our relationship, our love affair, with Christ.* Such a love is sterile and joyless.

We may not even be aware of our deep problem: our lack of a joy-filled relationship with Christ. And I think one of the ways this problem stands out most vividly is the way so many believers approach the issue of discipleship. It is presented as an intense experience but primarily *intellectual*. It calls for commitment, but essentially it is a commitment to reason and apologetics. It challenges, but it lacks a passion and joy of the heart. As a result, discipleship is essentially about working for God.

AN INCREDIBLY ADVENTUROUS
AND PASSIONATE JOURNEY

Abraham of the Old Testament left his country and people. He left his relatives and friends to follow an outlandish promise from a God he had only just met. He never turned back!

Jacob ended up losing everything he had worked his whole life for. He found himself wrestling all night on the muddy banks of the Jabbok because he had decided to pursue a passionate relationship with God.

Peter left everything he had to follow a Savior who wouldn't let him simply settle for fishing. And in the process, impetuous Peter found himself involved in a passionate pursuit of epic proportions.

Every one of these men and hundreds more found in the pages of God's love letters—the Bible—found themselves caught up in this passionate pursuit of the heart. Frequently, they changed their pattern of employment and place of residence. These fundamental transitions reflected the fact that they had been called to a radical change of heart. They were called to the romance of discipleship, a journey of determined intimacy to a purity of heart.

As you look closely at God's love letters, you come to realize a fascinating fact: These folks weren't the ones ultimately doing the pursuing—it was always God who pressed the issue.

Abraham wasn't wandering around looking for God. Instead, God showed up with an invitation and a challenge. Jacob was busy dealing from the bottom of life's deck, working on his recent pyramid scheme, when God showed up and promised him a whole new life. Peter was always cussing and fishing, or fishing and cussing. The guy was a rotten fisherman. I have read through the entire New Testament in the original language and not once does the text say Peter managed to catch anything on his own. He was the original dipstick for God. He is my kind of guy! Then Andrew, his brother, shows up and drags him to meet Jesus.

Discipleship is ultimately about the decision of whether or not we will respond. Will we accept this invitation to an incredible romance? Will we open our hearts to God's joy-filled presence?

> *Discipleship is ultimately about whether or not we will respond— Will we open our hearts to God's joy-filled presence?*

ROMANCE IN A FALLEN WORLD

As anyone who is married has discovered, just because you are loved by someone doesn't automatically mean everything is going to turn out wonderful. Discipleship is no exception to this rule. Yes, you are loved and pursued by God, but discipleship is about romance in a *fallen world*. That truth is why it is so easy for us to pull away from one another in marriage, in friendships and especially in our relationship with God.

In fact, it is especially easy for us to respond to God by pulling back, because He is perfect, all knowing, all powerful, sovereign and, above all, holy. That is why it is common for us to fall into a pattern of living with a hesitant heart toward God in the tough times.

The predominant stories of our lives are not the headlines in the newspapers or the awards and plaques we may have displayed in our office. The real story is not the external story;

instead, it is the story of the journey of the heart. If we live with our eyes fixed on the external, at some point we will lose track of our heart.

That is precisely why the statement Paul made in Philippians 3 is not just a summary of his life but the reason for his greatness. These words are a magnificent picture of a bold heart:

> I want to know Christ and the power of his resurrection and the fellowship of sharing in his sufferings, becoming like him in his death, and so, somehow, to attain to the resurrection from the dead (vv. 10-11).

Paul is not crying out for mere intellectual knowledge. His choice of words in the original is very specific. He wants to know Christ in the fullness of experiential knowledge, which is worked within us only as we become more like the lover of our soul. Paul hungers to know the fellowship—the participation in the sufferings of Christ. He refers not to the sufferings of Christ on the cross but to Christ's disciples, who will go through suffering for righteousness' sake. Suffering is the process whereby we experience healing and have our lives made whole and right with God.

Draw Close to God Before You Feel the Heat

Have you discovered that *pain* plays an important role in the process of getting healed? That is why so many folks don't move toward healing until their roof collapses on them. Getting healed emotionally, relationally and spiritually is what real discipleship is all about.

I remember the first time I realized what my addictions were doing to me. I had just pulled off a target, having dropped bombs at an extremely low altitude to keep some of our troops on the ground alive. I had been at that altitude for two reasons.

First, the battle on the ground was nose to nose, so I had to get low to pick out the right noses. And second, the weather ceiling was so low that I couldn't drop from the normal altitude. As I pulled off the target, I was immediately in trouble because I had pressed in so low to the ground. The surrounding mountain suddenly came rushing up to meet me. I felt the plane shudder as I pulled up as hard as I could. The plane started to stall despite the high speed. The jungle canopy was no longer a green blur; it seemed like I could count individual leaves. In an act of desperation, I stomped on the rudder pedals and slid the plane between two mountain peaks. Once I stopped inhaling my oxygen mask and calmed down, I realized some things that really terrified me: I wasn't even strapped in and I wasn't locked into the ejection seat. In my hungover state, I had climbed into the aircraft and failed to follow basic safety procedures.

I finally faced the fact that if I didn't change, my love for alcohol was going to kill me. I had almost ejected from the aircraft, which would have killed me. And in my hungover state, my reaction time was so hindered that I could easily have killed some of our own troops. It was a painful moment for me to admit how messed up I was.

Another painful episode was the time I woke up to the way my anger was wounding my wife and little girl after I returned from Vietnam. The pain of realizing what I was doing was devastating. Yet the truth is, most of us don't see the light until we feel the heat.

Paul cried out in Philippians 3:10-11, "I want to . . . attain to the resurrection from the dead." He isn't wondering if he will be physically resurrected or not, because in 1 Corinthians 15 he clearly states his confidence in that fact. Instead, he uses a unique word found only one time in the New Testament. It literally means, "out resurrection."[1] He wants the resurrection lived out in his life. He wants to live for God here and now—not when things start to look grim but all the time.

Don't Settle for Cheap Substitutes

I have lived life long enough to realize there is only one thing that I deeply fear—and it isn't death. My fear is that when I sense the death angel's presence preparing me for the journey home, I will lie there wondering what would have happened if only I had . . . I fear not death but indecision. I fear failing to fully experience and express God's purpose and plan for my life, hesitating at some point to risk it all for Christ. I fear I will not live my life with a bold heart like Paul did, choosing instead to medicate my inner wounds instead of facing them. Oh, not with alcohol, pornography and anger like I used to do, but I would choose acceptable, Christian addictions like overworking, religious performance, conformity, overeating or whatever—there are thousands of options. My fear is that I will miss the incredible joy of discipleship and settle for some cheap substitute.

LIFE WITH A BOLD HEART

Living the kind of life that Paul talked about—a life that truly knows the joy Christ referred to in John 17—*is not easy*. I think Forrest Gump expressed the frustration of many folks in the hit movie *Forrest Gump*. As he stood at the foot of Jenny's grave, he pensively commented, "I don't know if we each have a destiny, or if we are all just floating around accidental-like on a breeze."

That question continually haunts the movie. It is the nagging fear that lies behind all the humor—that our lives are nothing more than a feather caught by the wind. Even believers can end up feeling like a feather in the wind. They have heard the wondrous invitation to the adventure of discipleship from the heart of God, but soon the wounds and pain of living in a fallen world begin to hinder them, and they feel caught in a dilemma. They are caught between trusting in God's joy and trusting in their surrounding circumstances. The ongoing litany in their soul sounds something like this:

> If God is gracious and passionate toward me, then why are all these things slamming into my life? Should I play the perfect Christian game of denial and pretend that everything is wonderful? Or should I whine that life ought to be better than this? Yet if I focus on my wounds, I end up letting them define who I am. And if they become the determining word in my life, despair and anger become my ultimate destination. I can't live pretending everything is wonderful either—it isn't!

But unlike Forrest Gump, Scripture tells us that we stand before an empty tomb. Our hope is in a risen Savior. We are not floating through life like a feather in the wind of circumstance.

Understanding the Power of the Cross

In 2 Corinthians, Paul tells us he was shipwrecked in the open ocean three times, frequently took dangerous journeys and was beset by hostile hyperreligious folks and feisty Gentiles. False believers pursued him in the city, country and on the sea. It is a wonder the guy was able to get up and head to the office on Monday morning!

His life story is a sequence of one setback or put-down after another. The Corinthian church openly told everyone who would listen that Apollos was a much better preacher than Paul—and a lot better looking to boot. All of this didn't seem to bother Paul deeply, because he had this amazing ability to see

God's work in the midst of his own apparent failures. He truly understood the power of the Cross.

The Cross for us, however, can become a religious symbol that we cherish or a point of doctrinal truth we defend against all the assaults of humanism. Yet it is neither; instead, it is the doorway through which all of us must pass if we are ever going to experience the deep joy Christ prays for us to have.

Knowing Discipleship Will Be Tough at Times

I love the story of the little boy reading an exciting adventure novel. His hero, a daring young aviator, was in serious trouble. Everything was falling apart. The bad guys were closing in to shoot him down. The little guy couldn't stand the suspense any longer, so he did what you have done many times—he turned to the end and read the last chapter. His hero was able to pull the plane out, shoot down all the bad guys and fly off into the sunset with his sweetheart. Then the little boy turned back to where he had been previously reading; and when things started to get grim, he told the hero, "Don't worry. Don't panic. It's going to turn out great!"

My point? The Holy Spirit always tells us the same thing if we have ears to hear: "It is going to be rough, but I will be faithful. If you could only see as I see. If you only knew what I know." That is why intimacy—closeness with God—brings a boldness of heart.

In Acts 9, we read of Paul's initial calling and commissioning by the Holy Spirit. He is promised a wonderful ministry. God is going to have him speaking before kings and rulers. But it also is going to be tough at times. A true promise from God will *always* contain two elements:

1. Your life will be used greatly.
2. It is going to be tough at times.

Now that truth is huge! It is critical for you to understand that this is going to be a great adventure. Yet, at the same time, this discipleship thing really can get tough. There will be setbacks. There will be disappointments. There will be failures. Knowing this is critical. Paul understands that these challenges are part of the process. They are part of having a great marriage, a great family, a great ministry or a great business. But more important, Paul understands the need to trust and not to panic. He knows the end of the story—it is going to come out great!

Accepting Discipleship as Unique to the Individual

Peter stands on the shore of the Sea of Tiberias, or the Sea of Galilee, in John 21. He is dripping wet, and as usual, his impulsiveness is writing checks his character can't cash. Jesus is telling him his fishing days are finished, that he is going to pastor people. The incredible promise Christ initially uttered over him when they first met is now being affirmed and released. But as I pointed out, every great promise from God comes with a promise and a problem at the same time. Picture the possible conversation between Peter and Jesus at this moment:

> "Peter, you no longer do just what you want to do, and tough times are coming," says God.
>
> Peter begins to grasp the holiness of Christ at a whole new level. "Peter, things are really going to change," he is told. "Up to now you kind of called the shots and had lots of opinions, but it is not going to be that way anymore. This is about determined intimacy."
>
> Then Peter notices John walking along carefree and happy behind them. He asks, "Ah, pardon me, Lord, I am all for this discipleship thing. I know it is going to be challenging and at times rough, and that is fine, but, ah,

I don't know how to ask this, but does John get the same deal as I do? I don't mind it being tough at times just as long as it is equally tough on everyone else."

 *Every great promise from God comes with a promise and a problem at the same time.*

One of the most confusing things about personal pain—a problem that can suck God-given joy out of us like nothing else—is the issue of equity. At times we can look around us and see all kinds of folks who appear to be having the time of their life while we are getting buried. The most encouraging aspect of healing, restoration and small groups we have at East Hill is that people discover they are not the only ones on the planet with a particular problem. When a cocaine addict, someone caught in sexual bondage, a lady confessing multiple abortions, or a man or woman eaten alive with anger finally realizes he or she is seated in a group of folks struggling with the exact same problem, real healing begins.

When we don't realize our pain and struggles are common to the human race, we can become extremely vulnerable and susceptible to putting our hope in some lover other than God to meet our deepest needs. Or we can choose some form of immediate gratification to hide the pain within. It may be an affair, an obsession with sports, work, pornography, food or the pursuit of the elusive romantic illusion of the perfect person.

One night Diane and I were sitting around the table after dinner talking to our daughter, Nikki, who was starting high school. Nikki commented, "Dad, I want to marry someone just like you." My chest began to expand with pride until my wife looked at her and said, "Honey, they don't come that way. You have to train them!" So much for finding the perfect person.

If we think we will find the ultimate answer to our struggles and fears through someone or something other than God, we set ourselves up for even more pain. I have spoken to thousands of men about their struggles with sexual issues. A comment that G. K. Chesterton made years ago has turned on more lights of understanding than just about anything else I could ever say:

> Everyone who knocks on the door of a brothel is looking for God.[2]

GNATS AND NUCLEARS

I know some of you must be saying right now, "Well, Ted, it sure doesn't feel like it is going to come out great." That is because we misunderstand the purpose of God-given gnats and nuclears in our life.

The Nagging Pests

The gnats are those things that just keep hitting us, nibbling at us and pestering us over and over again. But if your heart is like Paul's—to know Christ—the Lord will point out what this pattern of gnats reveals about your soul. The gnats frequently reflect a paradigm of wounding from our past. That is why discipleship is not so much a pattern of *adding* discipline; instead, it is what Christ has been *pointing* us toward for years.

We have a standing joke in our family: When Dad tries to fix something, we end up having to hire someone to come and fix the fix. I have chuckled about this issue for years and responded by saying, "Hey, I don't fix 'em, I just fly 'em." But behind the chuckle lies a point of pain. Every now and then, that pain has poked out its ugly head and expressed itself in anger.

One day I was working on fixing something in the bathroom. As I worked on the broken plumbing, my wife walked in. She tried to encourage me by asking how I was doing. Without even thinking, I fired an angry response at her. She simply turned around and walked out the door. I knew where she was headed. She was going to talk with God. And that meant I was in big trouble! When she ducks and doesn't react to my anger, God steps in and deals with me big-time.

As I continued to work on the feisty piece of plumbing, frantically trying to think up a justification for my stupid comment, she walked back in and simply said, "Have you ever noticed when you work on the house you get upset easily?" She turned around and walked out again.

I sat there in stunned silence. She was right. I had been dealing with that particular gnat of anger all our married life. Being raised in an alcoholic home with seven stepfathers, I had never had a dad show me how to fix anything. That is why I always felt like a fool when I tried to fix anything around the house. Yes, I know that doesn't make any sense, but gnats are not about logic; they are about loss. In order to live with a bold heart, I needed to deal with my personal pain and confront the gnat.

The Big Whammies

The nuclear times are when *everything* gets leveled. The doctor's report comes back with the big c-word attached to it. I have been there. I have counseled many individuals who had been given that diagnosis, but it feels totally different when someone says *you* have cancer.

You lose your job. Your mate announces they are leaving.

The nuclear times in life expose your deepest fears. And hell will always show up to announce the fact that you are finished. Yet it is in the nuclear times we are given a unique gift. It is there, as nowhere else, we decide whether or not we believe the end of our story as God defines it—that it is going to come out great.

It is such a critical time in our life, because it is in the nuclear times when all of *our* joy is blown away that we find out if *His* joy is present in our lives. As the airplane illustration points out, the discipleship experience is a dynamic balance and tension. Christ prays for six different elements to be in dynamic balance in our lives. The first two are joy and holiness. Our joy will be shallow and based solely on human emotion unless it is connected to the holiness of God. Christ prayed that *His* joy might be in us and increase. Therefore, if we connect to God's holiness, then by default, *His* joy in us will increase.

PERSONALIZATION OF OUR CALLING

At times there does seem to be disparity in life, but if you have said yes to Christ, your life is "Father filtered." These moments come your way for two reasons. First, Christ wants to draw you to Himself. It is why you are going through what you are going through. It is why you feel so alone. He is calling you to Himself. He wants just the two of you to be together. You don't have to take a number and stand in line. It is a personal invitation from the lover of your soul.

Second, over a period of time you will notice a pattern as Christ personalizes His call in your life. Paul at the beginning of the most pain-filled book he wrote declares:

> Praise be to the God and Father of our Lord Jesus Christ . . . who comforts us in all our troubles, *so that we*

can comfort those in any trouble with the comfort we ourselves have received from God (2 Cor. 1:3-4, emphasis added).

Personal pain and struggles are always part of a true, God-given vision. The burden always precedes the vision when it is from God. There is a simple reason for that order—the burden purifies our motives. However, most folks desire to have a God-given vision first. But God seldom works that way.

A WORD TO THE WISE

Maybe I can sum everything up with this obvious truth: My precious friend, it is time to be bold and rejoice, despite your disappointment. It is time to wholeheartedly believe God once again. If you have any doubts, read the end of the book, like the little boy reading the adventure novel. We win! Revelation tells us it is a rigged game for those who have said yes to Christ. We win in Christ!

 *We win! Revelation tells us it is a rigged game for those who have said yes to Christ.*

"But, Ted, you don't know what I have been through." And you are right. I don't know. But God does! More important, He knows the end of your story. He knows what He has planned for you. And it is always good.

Guess what? God is opening a door for you right now despite the pain. God has set an open door before you—an outrageous invitation to a lifelong romance that steps right into eternity—a door that swings wide as you learn to walk in *His* joy. It is time to get up and walk out into His blessing and provision for you!

Let's complete your analysis of the joy factor of discipleship, continued from chapter 3. Read each statement and circle the number that best corresponds to your answer.

6. I find it highly irritating to have to help other people with their personal struggles.

Most of the time		Sometimes		Not at all
1	2	3	4	5

7. I am confused at times about God's purpose and plan for my life.

Most of the time		Sometimes		Not at all
1	2	3	4	5

8. I can easily see God at work in the midst of my failures.

No, it is a struggle		Sometimes		Yes
1	2	3	4	5

9. I believe God wants to use my life greatly, even when things get really rough.

No	I am confused at times			Yes
1	2	3	4	5

10. I have a good grasp of God's calling on my life.

No	Sometimes			Yes
1	2	3	4	5

Score _____ (Add together the numbers you circled.)
Enter score from chapter 3 _____
Total score _____ (Add together the scores from chapters 3 and 4.)

Take this total score for Joy and enter it in the appropriate space on the Discipleship Development Analysis Tool in chapter 12.

CHAPTER FIVE

A HEART FOR HOLINESS

Fall in Love with God

> *I have given and communicated Your Word to* [put your name here]
> *and my other disciples. As a result, the world has hated them,*
> *because they haven't joined the world's way of thinking and living,*
> *just as I am not of the world.*
> (SEE JOHN 17:14.)

Our astronomy class had been invited to an observatory in western Washington to view celestial objects we had been studying. It turned out to be a perfect night, and amazingly enough, the telescope was not being used for research projects. Our focus was the Crab Nebula.

The Crab Nebula is a star remnant that exploded into a

supernova in A.D. 1054. The luminosity of the star increased by 500 million times during the explosion. Chinese observers of the time even saw it during the day for three weeks.

Several times the mass of our sun, the star exploded from the inside out, leaving a remnant whose mass is so dense that one pinhead of its matter would weigh 1 million tons.[1] The gas cloud from the eruption has been traveling outward at 50 million miles a day ever since, leaving behind a fiery trail of gas and matter throughout the galaxy.

As the students peered through the telescope's viewing lens, their initial response was stunned silence, and then "Wow!" Afterward, an interesting thing took place. The class spontaneously gathered together and broke into worship, amazed such a wonder could exist. However, you can take that response and multiply it times infinity when it comes to the *holiness of God*!

Astronomers now have been able to look back through space and time to the very first microsecond of existence. They have discovered that everything that *is* was contained in a rapidly expanding spark of energy smaller than the nucleus of an atom. But they can go no further, because they have reached the absolute limits of the laws of science and physics. As Dr. Jastrow, a theoretical physicist, professor and writer involved with NASA's lunar exploration, observed, scientists find themselves standing with men and women of faith who have been standing there for thousands of years[2]—and I would add, lifting up praise to a holy God. The holiness of God may be a foreign concept in today's world, but what we have seen is a profound part of Christ's prayer for us.

GOD IS THE ALPHA AND THE OMEGA

Moses asked God, "Who are you?" (see Exod. 3:13). God's

response must have deeply puzzled him: "I am who I am" (Exod. 3:14). Not too long ago I had the opportunity to travel to Brazil, Australia and the East Coast of the United States. As a creature limited by time, I have to use all of those complicated verb tenses to describe my relationship to time. God doesn't; He just says, "I am."

In God's profound "Amen-ness," you are dealing with a being that has no beginning and no end. He is unchanging and unchangeable. Let your mind honestly wrestle with that reality for a while, and you will be brought to one place—worship.

God has chosen to reveal Himself as being holy. Of all the characteristics of God expressed in the Bible, holiness is mentioned more often than any other. But for most folks today, the term "holy" isn't awe inspiring. It even can be used in a negative way: "He is a holy roller" or "Don't try to be holier than thou."

When God uses the term to describe Himself in Scripture, it is to declare the very nature of His being. Isaiah declares, "To whom, then, will you compare God?" (Isa. 40:18). There is no one to compare with Him. He is something else!

I was watching highlights of our local NBA team (the Blazers), and the announcer was shouting, "What an awesome dunk." I was thinking, *I could dunk a basketball like that if they gave me a high enough stepladder.* I admit it was an impressive highlight. As the player flew through the air, deftly avoiding defenders and pulling off a reverse dunk, the crowd went nuts. That is nothing compared to what God can do. God could slam-dunk our galaxy!

Now that's impressive. Now we're talking about the awesome holiness of God. And here is the most incredible fact of all—Jesus specifically prayed for us:

I have given and communicated Your Word to [put your name

here] *and my other disciples. As a result, the world has hated them, they haven't joined the world's way of thinking and living, just as I am not of the world. I am not just praying for those surrounding Me tonight, but also for those who will come to believe and trust in Me through their witness, so they would all be of one heart and one mind just as You, Father, are in Me and I in You* (see John 17:14,20-21).

What a declaration—if we believe, the holy One resides in us!

IT'S ALL ABOUT GOD'S LOVE FOR US

One of the things I love about Paul's writings is the way in which he takes the holiness of God and relates it to the struggles of our daily existence. In Philippians 2:12-13, he says "Continue to work out your salvation with fear and trembling, for it is God who works in you to will and to act according to his good purpose." What a marvelous expression of the tensions of God's holiness and our fallen nature, of His grace and our neediness. But how do we work this out? Paul makes it clear in Philippians 4:6-7:

Do not be anxious about anything, but in everything, by prayer and petition, with thanksgiving, present your requests to God. And the peace of God, which transcends all understanding, will guard your hearts and your minds in Christ Jesus.

To be anxious is a familiar emotion for human beings. It is concern about something that hasn't happened yet. It is fear of the future. It is being tormented by the report from the doctor. The agony over losing your job. The stress of what might happen in your marriage or to your child. But Paul tells us in "every-thing," not just some things, we are to call out to our heavenly Father. Mention everything to Him. Bring the anxious thoughts to His attention, because He knows the future. He is present in your present, was present in your past and will be present in your future.

In verse 7, Paul goes on to say that if we respond to life in light of who God is and do not allow our problems to define us, we will receive an awesome peace. It is a crazy peace—a peace that doesn't make sense to our totally time-limited mind. It is a peace not based on how we feel; instead, it is a response to the presence of a holy God within us! *His holiness allows us to have peace in the midst of the pressures of life.*

Transform Your Thought Life

Paul doesn't stop there, because life is not easy at times. It is important to realize our thought life will always determine where we end up in life. With the skill of a master surgeon of the soul, Paul continues and cuts to the core of our inner battles:

> Finally, brothers, whatever is true, whatever is noble, whatever is right, whatever is pure, whatever is lovely, whatever is admirable—if anything is excellent or praise-worthy—think about such things. Whatever you have learned or received or heard from me, or seen in me—put it into practice. And the God of peace will be with you (Phil. 4:8-9).

Paul's point is clarion clear. God's peace in our lives is released once we change the way we think. Everything that sur-rounds you right now, as you read this book, started out as a thought. The universe, the sun, the moon, the earth—all of creation—started in the mind of God. God spoke—and it was. Mankind has a God-given capacity to create as well. The chair you are seated in, the lamp you may be reading by, the home you are residing in—all of them started out as a thought in someone's mind. Paul points out that you are furnishing your mental home with thoughts as well. That is why true discipleship and spiritual growth are only possible when we accept the fact that Christ is praying for us. Specifically, He is praying that we would understand He *has already made* us one with Him and the Father. Only when we accept the fact that *Christ has already made possible an intimate relationship with the Father can we grow in holiness and wholeness.*

Believe in God's Love

Often I have counseled individuals who have never realized that it is not what we do that ultimately determines who we are; it is who we believe we are that determines what we do. Too many believers are trying to be Christians by the way they live. Character and integrity are very important, but listen carefully: This approach will never work. It will not bring a sense of peace in your life. Paul tells us in Romans 8:15: "For you did not receive a spirit [of bondage] that makes you a slave again to fear." In other words, coming to Christ isn't trading one type of performing for another.

Instead, we have received a spirit of adoption that prompts our heart to cry out "Daddy, Father God." Our ultimate challenge *is to believe what God says about us is true and to live by faith in that fact.* Then, His holiness can give us a powerful perspective in the pandemonium of a fallen world.

"But, Ted, isn't that totally throwing aside any sense of discipline? How can we ever become disciples of Christ?" Paul brings a beautiful balance to the discussion:

Whatever you have learned or received or heard from me, or seen in me—put it into practice. And the God of peace will be with you (Phil. 4:9).

Once we understand how outrageously we are loved in Christ and catch a glimpse of God's holiness, then we can act effectively. We will be able to truly move toward wholeness with a determined intimacy. Then and only then can we become pure-hearted disciples. This is not a three-step process; instead, it is a continuous learning and growth cycle we will go through for the rest of our short time here in this world.

> *The foundation of Christian love is not the will to love but the faith to believe we are deeply loved of God.*

At some point, we discover the majesty and nature of Christ in a deeper sense. Then we hear His words of grace to us, defining who we really are. And out of that, we step forth into action, which brings us to a deeper discovery of how majestic He is! The foundation of Christian love is not the will to love but the faith to believe we are deeply loved of God.

Christ's ordering of the greatest commands in Matthew 22:36-39 points out that love begins with God. Also, our transformation into wholeness and holiness doesn't begin with us trying to love others more deeply. It isn't created by us trying to love ourselves more fully. It begins and ends with us falling outrageously in love with God.

TRAINING IS MORE THAN JUST TRYING HARDER

Falling in love with God is not an easy process, because for most of us, we literally have to carve out brand-new ways of thinking while the enemy fights us every inch of the way. To succeed in winning the battle of the mind, we need to heed the Holy Spirit's call to training. And that doesn't mean just trying harder.

Stay Fit

Spend your time and energy in the exercise of keeping spiritually fit. Bodily exercise is all right, but spiritual exercise is more important and is a tonic for all you do (see 1 Tim. 4:7-8).

I am hoping to pull off an Ironman Triathlon—2.4-mile swim, 112-mile bike and 26.2-mile run—in the near future. Now, I'm not crazy enough to just show up at the starting line without ever having spent any time training. That would be an exercise in total frustration. Paul points to the analogy of physical training with respect to our spiritual life. We must train to be effective both spiritually and physically.

For example, we might hear a great sermon about being patient and promise ourselves that tomorrow we are going to try really, really hard. We will discover that approach is a recipe for total failure. Trust me, it doesn't work. My point: Significant spiritual change in our lives involves training in God's love, not just trying really hard. In fact, much like training for a triathlon, you will have to rearrange your life to include certain training activities that by the grace of God will enable you to do what you presently cannot do.

Break the Pattern

One year I signed up for a summer camp to learn how to swim effectively in open water races. Immediately, I had to battle with the fact that I had never learned how to swim correctly. I was thrashing through the water. I was fighting the water. An easy problem to fix, right? Wrong. The pattern literally was burned into my brain after years of repetition. The stressful situation rapidly went from bad to worse as several hundred other folks testing the waters swam over the top of me. The fear of drowning was constantly in the back of my mind.

Many people I have counseled over the years felt like they were drowning emotionally, relationally or spiritually. Their problems were always rooted in the patterns that had been deeply burned into their brain years before. They loved God and wanted to follow and obey him, but they were still drowning because they only were trying harder—they had no training program.

These patterns can be particularly strong where sexual events are concerned. When we experience a strong emotional event in our lives, the brain underlines it chemically.[3] At the very least, the autonomic system triggers the release of chemicals in the brain to imprint the event. That is why Scripture refers to mental strongholds hell can form in our lives (see 2 Cor. 10:5). And that is why some individuals can be caught in sexual sin from childhood. They never seem to break the pattern no matter how hard they try. Obviously, these strongholds are not just limited to sexual issues. There can be a fear of authority figures, anger issues, codependency, hyperconcern about money or food, relational blind spots—you name it. However, we will devote the rest of the chapter to exposing one of our deadliest patterns—sexual strongholds.

A Man's Battleground for Wholeness Is Unique

I doubt there is a clearer battleground for men today with respect to wholeness and holiness than sexuality. In the last few years, I have had the privilege of speaking to numerous men's gatherings. Because of my previous book *Pure Desire* (Regal Books, 1999), I am frequently asked to address the subject of men's sexual struggles. It is no longer unusual to see 70 to 85 percent of the men come forward at the end of the message to acknowledge their struggles with masturbation and other sexual issues.

You might be asking why I have suddenly turned from talking about God's holiness to men's struggle with their sexuality. The reason is very simple: The vast majority of men who step forward at these events are sincere believers. They are tired of trying harder. They cry out for God's holy touch on their lives, but they don't feel this presence.

Now, ladies, I ask you to hang in there with me for two reasons. First, the fact so many men are struggling means you may end up relating to a man who is battling with this issue. Second, the issue is much larger than just one man's conflicts. In the Old Testament, there is a warning God gave His people before they entered the Promised Land:

> Do not defile yourselves in any of these ways [God has just listed a litany of sexual sins the people of the land are involved in], because this is how the nations that I am going to drive out before you became defiled. Even the land was defiled; so I punished it for its sin, and the land vomited out its inhabitants. For all these things were done by the people who lived in the land before you, and the land became defiled. *And if you defile the land, it will vomit you out as it vomited out the nations that were before you* (Lev. 18:24-25,27-28, emphasis added).

The issue of godly men and women walking in His guidelines with respect to sexual purity is not just one of personal responsibility and accountability. Disobedience can bring about a sequence of events that leads to the eventual destruction of a nation. If you read through the sexual practices listed in Leviticus 18, they read like the front page of your morning newspaper. America is involved in the very same practices. I honestly believe as a nation we are also moving toward a danger zone defiling our land.

Therefore, this issue in the vast majority of men's lives in the Church has to be effectively and graciously healed. Otherwise, our kids and grandkids could grow up in an absolutely hellish environment.

Unless we have a real revival—not just a get-happy time for believers—our nation is headed for some dire consequences. Unless there is a transformation of the moral character of our nation, it won't matter how many megachurches we have, how many people say yes to Christ, how many new churches are planted and how many evangelistic campaigns we hold—they will just be a window dressing. If the holiness of God doesn't penetrate the moral fibers of our nation through the transformed lives of passionate followers of Christ, then we are in deep trouble as a society. Unless there is an explosive growth of pure-hearted disciples of Jesus in our land, unless men who love the Lord can win this battle for sexual purity, the future looks rather bleak.

"Ted, don't you think that is an overstatement?" you may be asking. No, it really isn't, because a sexual habit such as masturbation—a dominant sexual stronghold men face—and other sexual fantasies are always the entrance to much deeper sexual bondage and addictions.[4] It is impossible to walk in a growing sense of wholeness and holiness with these kinds of activities going on behind the scenes in a person's life.

But here is the good news: Once men realize how they can

win this battle and begin to walk it out in their lives in a practical way, then the holiness of God will finally make sense to them. Then they can believe Christ's loving words. They will begin to understand that Jesus doesn't just love some spiritual or eternal part of them—He loves *all of them.*

God's goal in all of our lives is not for us to become less human and more divine; His heart is for us to become more fully human. Jesus embraced our humanity in His incarnation. That should tell us something about how He values it. To become like Jesus, we need to embrace not only His character but also our humanness. Honest, nonreligious spirituality is the redemption of our humanity, not a denial or crucifixion of it. Scripture calls us to crucify our flesh, but that is referring to our self-centeredness and our attempts to live apart from God's will (see Gal. 2:20). Our body is not our real problem. Our struggle is with our soul, heart and mind, which express our pains, fears and addictions. Saint Irenaeus expressed it best when he declared that the glory of God is a fully alive human being.[5]

WINNING THE BATTLE IS NECESSARY TO BE A FULLY ALIVE HUMAN BEING

Most surveys of sexual behavior reveal that over 95 percent of young men at some point in their lives have masturbated. After speaking to thousands of men, I think the other 5 percent lied. But masturbation is not the unpardonable sin. The struggle we are addressing here is the habitual act of a sin. We'll use masturbation as an example, since it affects almost all men. The personal sense of shame that develops as a result of this practice is devastating to a man's spiritual life. He starts feeling dead on the inside. So how do you win the battle to become fully alive in

Christ? This plan of attack can apply to any habitual sin, whether it affects men or women or both.

How do you win the battle to become fully alive in Christ?

Step 1: We Must Understand That We Are Loved by God

Even in the deepest, darkest, most out-of-control times in our life, we need to understand God hasn't given up on us. Remember from our earlier discussion in this chapter, it is not what we do that ultimately determines who we are, but it is who we are that should determine what we do.

"But, Ted, I continue to do this very behavior I hate, despite the fact I have a loving wife and I love God with all my heart." My response is always the same: "You are in good company." In Romans 7 Paul tells us of a similar struggle:

> For I have the desire to do what is good, but I cannot carry it out. For what I do is not the good I want to do; no, the evil I do not want to do—this I keep on doing (vv. 18-19).

Paul graphically describes the pattern of being unable to delay immediate gratification—a struggle we all face at some point. He vividly expresses the frustrations of so many men I have counseled with respect to their sexual battles. God designed our sexuality as a gift, but when it's ruled by the quest for immediate satisfaction, then we find ourselves in the revolving door of defeat. I often try to get men's attention by telling them, "The difference between a boy and a man is a boy has to have what he wants right now. A man will choose to delay immediate gratification because of a higher cause." My point is that they usually are battling a pattern that began back in their early teens. It is a deep-seated mental pattern that drives the habitual, sinful responses in their life. They are not thinking as adults when it comes to sexuality.

The research occurring today with respect to the brain is amazing. Dr. Leis Judd, former director of the National Institute of Mental Health, commented:

> The pace of progress in neuroscience is so great that 90 percent of all we know about the brain we learned in the last ten years.[6]

Scientists have discovered that a child's brain at birth contains more than 100 billion neurons—that is nearly the number of stars in our galaxy. But the neurons are not what constitute our brain; rather, it is the connections between those nerve cells—the synapses.

The number of connections in a three-year-old's mind is truly colossal. There are up to 15,000 synaptic connections for each one of the 100 billion neurons. Yet by the time children reach their teenaged years, they only have one-half the synaptic connections they had as a three-year-old. Maybe that explains why your teenagers don't listen to you when you talk to them.

Why the drop in synaptic connections? Dr. Harry Chugani, professor of neurology at Wayne State University Medical School, describes it as a pruning process based on the frequency of usage. Mental highways that are repeatedly used broaden, but those rarely used fall into disrepair. Translation: The brain starts getting hardwired. That doesn't mean things can't change, but it is not an easy process.

"Wait a minute, Ted. What does all of this have to do with holiness and the love of God?" Would you believe *everything*! When mental patterns are so deeply engraved, such as being involved in masturbation for 25 years—which is quite common for Christian men I have counseled—the behavior is a habit, not just an occasional occurrence. Or think of a searing pattern formed in the mind of a young lady who was repeatedly abused by her father or someone close to her. I could enumerate a plethora of other painful experiences that are so much a part of our shattered society. My point: In our broken world today, the *love of God is our only hope*. We can receive counseling the rest of our life, but apart from a personal, powerful and profound encounter with the risen Christ and His Word, we won't have our mind renewed. The mental patterns will continue to haunt us; therefore, we must come to understand we are loved by God.

Step 2: We Must Change the Process of Our Sexual Behavior, Which Is Extremely Difficult

We literally have to carve new ways of thinking into our brain by the grace of God. The renewing of our mind, which Scripture refers to, can at times feel like we are carving a new road into the side of a granite mountain.

Sexual activity has a powerful effect on the brain which triggers the release of endorphins and encephala that give us the sense of a sexual high.[7] God designed this sexual high to be a blessing. It was created as a bonding process—a bonding to one person. In the Garden, God didn't bring a harem to Adam; He brought Eve. God configured our brain to work in such a way that after 20, 30, 40 years of marriage, we would be profoundly bonded to our mate. They become our sole desire. Have you ever seen a husband and wife who are both in their 70s that can't keep their hands off one another? That is God's plan; they are fully alive in Christ.

Let me put all these pieces of information together. Most men I have counseled regarding their sexual struggles have battled masturbation since their early teens. And now with Internet porn sites at work in kids' lives, the hellish mental highways of masturbation are being constructed at an earlier age. Once a young man is pulled down that highway, the sexual high can rapidly become the focus, not the relationship. That is why masturbation can become a deadly hook in the man's mind.

Step 3: We Have to Offer Our Brain and Body to God on the Altar of His Word

Now listen carefully: I am not asking the man to try harder religiously. The battle is in his mind. Will he believe he is deeply loved by God? Will he believe God's Word or the mental highways of his old thinking?

Let me summarize what I have said so far with another illustration. A few years ago, I was asked to speak to a group of pastors at a resort in Jackson Hole, Wyoming. The place was a fly fisherman's paradise. I was greeted at the crack of dawn with an incredible sight: The Tetons soared majestically in the distance, and a pristine trout stream stood before me, the early morning mist rising off the water's surface. I couldn't wait to get my trout line into the stream! But I spent the next half hour experiencing total frustration. I had never been fly fishing before, but I knew it couldn't be as hard as I was making it. I noticed a pastor further downstream catching fish as fast as he could. I waded downstream and asked if he could help me. He taught me two lessons I will never forget: Notice the insects the fish are feeding on, and then choose a fly that mimics the insects' appearance.

I had previously selected a huge purple and gold fly, thinking the brightness of the fly would attract the fish. The pastor gave me a tiny brown ugly-looking thing. He even tied it on for me, which was a lot better than my 500-pound granny knot. On the second cast, I hooked into a winner! I immediately started reeling in the fish. But my instructor warned me not to do that. "Let him run until the hook sets," he said. He took the rod and reel and showed me how it was done. With his finger lightly on the reel, he let the line play out. I asked him, "When should you reel the fish in?" "When the hook sets and he gets tired," the pastor said, smiling. I looked at the guy and thought, *This guy is just like the devil!*

The book of James would agree. In a masterful description of how sin hooks into our lives, James in chapter 1 tells us it starts with our going for the bait. The devil is a master destroyer of men. He watches carefully what we will feed on from our youth. Then with adroit craftiness, he places the fly of temptation before us. Once we take the bait, we have this line running out of our mind and soul. Over a few years, we can have an entire tackle shop from hell running out of the side of our soul. But the day comes—usually sooner than later—when hell sets the hook in our soul and mind, and we begin to bleed. Our family and our life bleed because of the secret in our mind and soul. I share this story because a lot of men I have helped didn't realize a deep hook had been set in their soul at an early age. They didn't understand that fact, and when they relapsed, they had been prepared to just quit and the hook only set deeper. This battle takes awhile!

Paul tells us we must offer our *body* and our *brain* to God (see Rom. 12:1-2). If we don't understand our brain, it will never work. In a very simplified sense, we have two critical parts to our brain with respect to our spiritual struggles. The first is the neocortex, which is located in the front part of our brain. It receives and stores information for decision making and remembering.

The second part lies deep inside the brain. It is the limbic system, which controls all the automatic systems of the body and the emotions, as well as the survival responses.[8] The limbic system doesn't know the difference between yesterday and 20 years ago, which explains why some of our childhood traumas and programming can affect us so powerfully today. Activities related to drugs, alcohol, sex and other compulsive behaviors can program the limbic system to avoid an awareness of uncomfortable thoughts instead of making healthy responses to fear, anger, loneliness and other negative emotions.

For example, I grew up in a home with seven stepfathers and an alcoholic mother. It was total chaos at times. I learned very early on that displaying any weakness or vulnerability could cost me dearly. It could result in anything from a public put-down, "Oh, toughen up, you wimp!" to a fist in the face. In order to survive day to day in such a hurting home, I developed a system of thought that allowed me to survive. Negative thoughts formed, such as, *If I don't need anybody, then I am not vulnerable. If I am not vulnerable, then I don't get hurt.* That system of thought may make sense in a deeply hurting home when you are a kid, but later it can make a marriage crazy.

When my wife would ask me to be vulnerable and open up, the old alarm bells would sound: Warning, warning, you will get killed! My instinctive thoughts for survival did almost kill our marriage. And guess what, it made me very vulnerable to a bondage of masturbation. When you are hurting and can't truly be vulnerable or intimate with anyone, then guess what you can count on to feel good—that's right, your old friend—masturbation. Many men don't have a clue how deep the battle they are fighting really goes. It is not just about what they do, but also it is about who they see themselves to be. It goes back to my first point—it ultimately is about realizing who you are in Christ. It's about believing God's Word.

Step 4: We Cannot Walk in God's Holiness Alone

This journey to become a pure-hearted disciple—the call to a lifestyle of determined intimacy—can never be taken alone. Yes, each of us must take our own journey and follow a unique pathway with Christ. But knowing God or ourselves cannot take place apart from others who are willing to give us input and a helping hand. Apart from my wife's constant pleas to open up, I would never have known just how locked up I was inside. The software within my mind and soul had been programmed in my brain so long ago that I didn't even notice it anymore. It was normal for me, yet it was affecting me negatively.

For us to truly respond to Paul's admonitions in Romans 12, we can't keep any secrets from those who are close to us. We are as sick as our secrets, which is precisely why every man who has said yes to Christ desperately needs a small group of men to totally open up with and to keep him accountable. I call my small group my climbing group. I can never reach the summit of Christ's wholeness and holiness for my life without them.

When it comes to breaking a long-term habit like masturbation, a small group is key to our freedom. In many ways, it's like we have had this little puppy in our life, and every time he messed on the floor, we threw him a porterhouse steak. After 10 or 20 years, this puppy isn't cute anymore. He has grown into a huge fat wolf, and the inner room of our life where that wolf lives is rather smelly, to put it nicely. Cleaning that mess up is not something we can easily do alone.

Step 5: We Need to Be Reminded Again of How Out-rageously God Loves Us—We Need to Come Full Circle

Our climbing group is crucial in communicating to us, especially if the pattern is deep. It usually is when we are dealing with a sexual struggle, which means we will find ourselves battling with relapse at some point in our discipleship growth. Jesus understood that very well, and that is why He prayed so passionately for us in John 17. Even though we have committed our life totally to Christ, uncovered the old lies and confronted them with

This journey to become a pure-hearted disciple can never be taken alone.

God's truth, there still will be a lag time between what our limbic system believes and what our heart and neocortex have learned is true. This is called the limbic lag.[9] It can be shorted if we continue to challenge the lies within by applying God's truth. We also must risk trusting others. Remember, it is a battle. It is the challenge that Paul refers to as the renewing of our minds—taking off the old and putting on the new (see Eph. 4:22-24).

One summer my wife and I visited Bermuda. We rented a scooter and drove around the island. I almost went nuts because in Bermuda they drive on the left side of the road. I came close to killing us every time we approached a traffic circle. I kept trying to go back to the old pattern of driving on the right side of the road, which would have put us into the path of oncoming traffic. The more stressful the intersection, the harder it was to remember. I had to really concentrate. In our stressful situations in life, we tend to revert to the old way of living. That is why we need a group of friends to help us steer back to the right side of the road whenever we veer off into oncoming traffic.

THE ROADWAY TO SUCCESS IS CHANGE

Change—real change—happens one decision at a time. It ultimately comes down to a decision to do the right thing, which is usually the hard thing. We must decide to do the right thing no matter how we feel and no matter how our software from the past screams at us. If we make that decision, Christ will supernaturally bless our efforts.

We are serving a holy God, and He is something else. He can take our efforts no matter how little they seem to us and do something absolutely awesome with them. He who could slam-dunk a galaxy will definitely slam-dunk hell's plans for our life, bringing us to a wholeness and holiness that we simply can't imagine.

Let's pause for a moment and reflect on your ability to experience God's holy presence in your life. Read each question or statement and circle the number that best corresponds to your answer.

1. At times have you been moved to worship simply because of the awesomeness of God?

Frequently		Occasionally		Infrequently
1	2	3	4	5

2. How often do you think about hurtful things from the past?

Frequently		Occasionally		Infrequently
1	2	3	4	5

3. Do you honestly believe that God is outrageously in love with you?

				At times I am overwhelmed
Not really		Somewhat		by that fact
1	2	3	4	5

4. With respect to spiritual disciplines like prayer, Bible study and attending services, are they a trial or do they feel like training?

				It's usually a discipline
I don't know		I'm confused at times		of delight
1	2	3	4	5

5. Do you feel that Jesus truly loves all of you—including your body?

				He truly
No		I'm not sure		loves all of me
1	2	3	4	5

6. Do you have any fishhooks in your soul that you are pulling against?

Several		A couple		Nothing is there
1	2	3	4	5

7. How hard is it for you to be fully vulnerable with those closest to you? (Ask your mate for confirmation on this one.)

Several		A couple		Nothing is there
1	2	3	4	5

8. I have a close group of friends or a climbing group that knows about all of my deepest struggles.

Not really		I'm getting there		Yes, indeed!
1	2	3	4	5

9. I have some secrets in my life.

Yes		A couple		Not one
1	2	3	4	5

10. How difficult is it for you to do the hard thing—the right thing—no matter how you feel?

It's a real battle		I struggle at times		I have learned to trust God, period
1	2	3	4	5

Score _____ (Add together the numbers you circled.) Take this total score for Holiness and enter it in the appropriate space on the Discipleship Development Analysis Tool in chapter 12.

Joy

Grace

Truth

Holiness

CHAPTER SIX

DRENCHED IN HIS GRACE

Becoming Pliable in Our Master's Hands

*My prayer is not that You pull them out of the world, but that You pro-
tect and guard them from the evil one. They are not defined by this
world, just as I am not defined by this world or a part of it.*

(SEE JOHN 17:15-16.)

My wife was speaking to a lady's group, and I thought it was the
least I could do to clean up after dinner. After all, she had done
all the cooking. I will admit this was an unusual experience for
me. I started looking for a sponge to help with the task. I finally
managed to find a well-used, crusty, dirty sponge. It was a rather
humble piece of equipment, not that useful, stiff as a board and
having a definite aroma. But when I put the sponge under the

cleansing flow of water, it changed in a matter of seconds. It became pliable. The embedded dirt was washed away, and more important, it became useful.

Sometimes our heart and life are like that sponge. We are dry, stale, inflexible and a bit smelly. We belong to the master of the house, but our usefulness is rather limited. Yet once we spend a few moments under the faucet of God's grace, something marvelous happens. As we allow His grace to pour over us, we become pliable. The junk is washed out of our life, and we become an effective tool in the hands of the master.

Which type of sponge are you? Unfortunately, that question is frequently viewed from such a religious- or performance-oriented perspective that it only makes us drier. But here is the good news, the grace news: We are only one request away from what God wants us to be. That is the incredible power of God's grace in our life. And above all, Christ is praying that the flow of His grace would protect and guard us from the evil one. As He declared in John 17, we are not defined by this world. It is not who we now are or who we have been that Christ sees with His gracious gaze; rather He sees who we desire to be. And even if we do not presently desire God above all else, we can *desire* to desire Him above all else; we can get under the flow of His grace and truth.

A RELATIONAL FATHER

We have come to the second set of truths that lie at the heart of Christ's discipleship prayer for us. Previously we looked at the relationship between joy and holiness, which only God can hold in perfect balance. Two truths that are more difficult at times to hold in dynamic tension are grace and truth. Grace without truth lacks a sense of purpose and destiny, and truth without grace lacks a sense of passion and delight.

D. L. Moody, one of the great evangelists in American history, is one of my heroes of the faith. He was converted as a shoe salesman; I sold shoes in high school and college. He began his ministry to the street kids of Chicago; I began my ministry in Teen Challenge, helping kids strung out on drugs.

One day two ladies in the church where Moody served came to him and told him they were praying he would be saturated with the Holy Spirit. Initially he was offended by the comment, but as his biography describes, soon he started hungering for the Holy Spirit's touch in his life:

> I began to cry as never before for a greater blessing from God. The hunger increase; I truly felt I didn't want to live any longer without it. I kept crying all the time that God would fill me with His spirit. One day in the city of New York—Oh, what a day—I cannot describe it. I seldom refer to it. It is almost too scary an experience to name. Paul had an experience of which he never spoke for 15 years. I can only say that God revealed Himself to me, and I had such an experience of His love.[1]

Later he wrote, "The love of God came on me wave after wave until I felt I would be crushed beneath the weight of God's kindness." He also commented, "I used to carry buckets, but now there is a river that carries me."[2]

I am convinced that D. L. Moody's experience is exactly the encounter with God's grace Jesus is praying for every believer to experience. Yet for so many that experience of grace is blocked because they don't know the Father. Christ's entire prayer in John 17 flows from a deep and passionate relationship with the Father.

A TEACHING FATHER

It is fascinating: The disciples had been with Jesus for months. They had seen Him heal the sick, raise the dead, even walk on water. But for the first time they asked Him, "Could you show us how to do that?"

> One day Jesus was praying in a certain place. When he finished, one of his disciples said to him, "Lord, teach us to pray" . . . He said to them, "When you pray, say: 'Father.'" (Luke 11:1-2).

Ever felt awkward in your initial comments to someone? You just didn't know what to say. I remember the first time I met my future father-in-law. Diane was staying at her parents' home for the weekend during college break. I showed up at the front door. I thought to myself, *What am I going to call her father? Sir? Big guy? Daddy of the gal that lights my fire?* I didn't know what to say, so I didn't say anything. I ended up standing in the living room waiting for Diane to get ready. Little did I know how many hours I would spend doing that in the years ahead.

Diane's brother was talking with his father about which major he should take in college. The options were engineering or mathematics. I jumped into the conversation: "Oh, you don't want to be an engineer; they're a bunch of dummies. All they do is plug numbers into formulas that math majors figure out. That is why I am a math major." That's right—Diane's father was an engineer for the California highways department!

The disciples were not just asking about the difficulty of talking to a father-in-law. They were struggling with how to address the creator of the heavens and the earth—the Lord God Almighty. Jesus responded by simply saying, "Call Him Father." That was one of the toughest hurdles I had to deal with in my initial walk with the Lord. It was difficult for me to refer to God as Father. With the parade of abusive and angry stepfathers I had in my life, the term "Father" didn't come easily to me in prayer.

> *The disciples were struggling with how to address the creator of the heavens and the earth— Jesus responded by simply saying, "Call Him Father."*

I doubt things were much different in the first century, which is why Jesus talked frequently about the Father. One of the most beautiful and important pictures Jesus ever presented of the Father was the parable of the prodigal son in Luke 15. If we are ever going to experience the depth of grace Christ is praying for us to know, then we must clearly see the source of that grace—God the Father.

Even if you are just investigating the claims of Christ, you are probably familiar with the parable. I want us to look at the story behind the story—the picture of the Father that is presented. We tend to focus on the prodigal, but the real heart of the story is the father.

A GIVING FATHER

You remember how the story begins—the youngest son comes to the father and asks for his inheritance, an unbelievable request in the culture of that time. If you really think about the son's request, the son was essentially saying, "Dad, I want to treat you as if you were dead. I don't want to be anything you are; I just want what you have." That was the only way the son could have received the inheritance in that day and age. Yet the father graciously gives his inheritance to him, even though there is a strong possibility the son will squander the gifts.

The amazing part is the *father does it*! He sells the car, the condo and the business. He cashes out the stocks, investments and bonds, and gives the money to his son. Jesus is telling us loud and clear, "When you think about God, I want you to think of a Father who is so giving that His generosity seems unimaginable."

Here is an interesting question: Have you ever had anyone treat you that way? It is an overwhelming experience. In the early years of our marriage, my wife did that for me. I was so totally focused on myself. I told her if it ever came down to a choice between airplanes and her, she would lose. She married me anyway, partly because she thought she could change me, but I only got worse. The first two years of our marriage she cried herself to sleep nearly every night. I didn't have a clue I was hurting her that deeply. She kept on loving and giving to me despite my self-centeredness—not out of codependency, but out of a sense of divine hope the Father had put in her heart for me. Her enduring love was one of the reasons I listened to her when she talked to me about Christ, and it was the main reason I responded to Christ in Vietnam when I read her love letter to me after my whole world had gone totally insane.

I don't know if you have ever felt that loved, but you are. Your heavenly Father will give to you, even when you squander what comes your way. Have you ever treated someone close to you—a friend, a mate, a gift from God—in a cavalier manner? Have you ever ignored what God has done for you and complained about not getting what you wanted? Have you ever pushed aside God's Word and done what you wanted to do? The answer to every one of those questions for anyone having a pulse is, "Yes, I have."

Jesus said, "When you think about God, think about a Father who has given and given to you." Even when you haven't been grateful or appreciative, you'll see He is awesome enough to handle our humanness and generous enough that at some point this will significantly change us.

Unmask the Fear

Jesus, the master storyteller, after setting the stage, presents in rapid-fire fashion the details of the disastrous choices of the younger son. The kid heads for the far country. He went for the wine, women and song. Today we would say he went for the cocaine, hookers and rave parties. Within a few months, he played out his streak. He is shipwrecked on the ragged rocks of total failure. He ends up working as a farm hand, slopping the hogs. Then a very predictable thing takes place: He comes to his senses and says, "How many of my father's hired men have food to spare, and here I am starving to death! I will set out and go back to my father and say to him: Father, I have sinned against heaven and against you. I am no longer worthy to be called your son; make me like one of your hired men" (Luke 15:17-19).

This is a graphic picture of a classic addict. He has just gone through a huge amount of money in a very short period of time. I often have seen individuals go through a great marriage, ministry or family in a brutally short period of time and end up in a pigpen in life. Like any addict who has been boxed in, he is scheming a way out in a matter of moments: *I know what I will do; I know what I will say to my father.* The parable tells us he is in the far country, so he has a lot of time to work on his spiel on the way home. So he starts constructing a slave's mask. All of us wear masks at times in relationships. Why do we do that? There is a one-word answer—fear. The first emotion that Adam and Eve experienced after the Fall was fear. It lies at the root of all our major relational problems. Fear makes it impossible for us to experience the grace of the Father that Jesus prays for us to know.

It is rather easy for us to wear a mask, because other people don't know what we are really like on the inside. Therefore, we can cover up what is within us. In fact, there is only one person in all the cosmos who truly understands you. And by the way, it isn't you. Only God the Father fully understands you and why you do what you do. Just ask your mate; they will tell you that about half the time you don't know what you're doing!

Face Your Hurts

In this world, you will be hurt and hurt again. The issue is what to do with your hurts. Will you rehearse them, hold on to them or hide them like the prodigal son tried to do? Those options are dead ends. We were meant to live life with courageous grace, which means we will have to take risks in life. Not many people do that very well. When the prodigal limped home, his motives were mixed at best. After a lengthy binge of waste and wandering, boozing and womanizing, he was going home just to survive. The wine had soured, the roses had wilted, and the money and his supposed friends were gone. He didn't come home out of a burning desire to see his father. He was, as the song puts it, "staying alive." And the trip from the far country always takes awhile. It is a sustained journey of putting one foot in front of the other. But at some point, if you keep at it, you will discover what the young man did.

AN EXPECTANT FATHER

I personally think that Luke 15:20 is one of the most beautiful and heart-gripping pictures of Father God presented in the Bible:

> But while he was still a long way off, his father saw him and was filled with compassion for him; he ran to his son, threw his arms around him and kissed him.

The original translation carries a sense that the Father kissed and kissed the boy. He slobbered all over him!

It is interesting to note the two things the father didn't do. The father was well connected. He probably knew exactly where the boy was all the time. Yet he didn't hop into his chariot and drive over to the pigpen and say, "All right, I have had just about enough of this. Get in the chariot, I'm taking you home." Not this dad. He knew the only thing the son had left was the dignity of choice. The very God to whom Jesus urges us to pray—our heavenly Father, who can release a flood of grace to wash through our lives—waits patiently for you and me. He doesn't push us around.

The father also didn't wipe his hands of the whole mess. Your heavenly Father waits patiently for you. He pays attention to your life. He scans the horizon of your possibilities, waiting for the slightest hint you are moving His way. In fact, a moment never goes by that God the Father doesn't have you on His mind. I love 1 Peter 5:7 in *The Living Bible*:

> Let him have all your worries and cares, for he is always thinking about you and watching everything that concerns you.

A SACRIFICIAL FATHER

Certain aspects of the parable take a bit of translation for us to get, because we see things from an American perspective. In the first century, men wore robes. It would have been a horrible offense for a man, especially an elder, to show his legs in public. Even when you travel to the Middle East today, it is not proper for a man to show his legs in public. You can pick out all the tourists at the historical sites—they are the ones wearing shorts.

A moment never goes by that God the Father doesn't have you on His mind.

This elder, this wealthy father, this dignified man *runs to his son*. He hikes up his robe and runs past all the servants, villagers and everyone in sight to get to his son. The farmer's fields would have surrounded the village; and as the son approached, he would have had to pass through the outskirts of town before he got to his father. The father had only two options: (1) he could let his son walk to him, having to face all the shame and the stares of the villagers; or (2) the father could run through the village and the gathering crowd, and take the shame upon himself.

The picture of Father God that Christ presents is absolutely stunning! The God of the universe sits enthroned in heaven—dignified, holy, awesome. But the moment we move toward Him, He races toward us. God could tell us we have to take the walk of shame, that we have to crawl on our knees to Him, but Jesus makes it very clear that God meets us where we are. He hikes up His royal robe and comes running to us, baring His legs in the process.

That is exactly what happened at the Cross. Christ was stripped naked and impaled on a savage Roman torture device. He was made a public spectacle—shamed, mocked, spat upon and laughed at. Have you ever wondered why Jesus went through all of that? If He died for our sins as the Bible declares, why did He go through all the shame and ridicule? The answer is simple and profound: so we wouldn't have to. The author of Hebrews expresses it best:

> Let us fix our eyes on Jesus . . . who for the joy set before him endured the cross, *scorning its shame*, and sat down at the right hand of the throne of God. Consider him who endured such opposition from sinful men, so that you will not grow weary and lose heart (12:2-3, emphasis added).

The Amazing Power of Forgiveness

The grace of God doesn't just mean we get what we don't deserve. It is much more amazing than that. The grace of God means forgiveness has preceded repentance in our lives. It did for the prodigal and it does for us too. Christ died for every sin we have committed, are presently committing and will ever commit. If we think we have to repent perfectly before God forgives us, then we don't understand the grace of God. We will either hide from God or end up being proud of our correct religious behavior. Either option is devastating, making it impossible to grow in a determined intimacy with the Lord.

Some might protest and say, "If you tell people that, then they will do whatever they want. They will go and sin like crazy, counting on God to forgive them." The Pharisees threw that same charge at the apostle Paul. And it is ridiculous, because if people truly meet Father God, they will only end up at one place—flat on their face in worship, lost in wonder and praise over the goodness and grace of God. *They come to realize that repentance isn't something they do in order to earn God's forgiveness; it's a heartfelt response of those who realize they have been forgiven!*

The Christ-Child Within Us

It is a sad but true fact that many of today's congregations would have baptized the prodigal son and immediately put him into an intense discipleship program rather than throw a party for him like the father did. They would probably say something like, "You need to be discipled. You must learn how to live correctly, how to live the Christian life. You must assume a certain persona." They would have totally missed the fact that real repentance and real transformation of the prodigal only took place after the party, only after he had experienced the father's grace.

I think something like this occurred at the father's breakfast table the next morning. The son turned to the father and said, "Father, I want your permission to go back to the far country someday soon. When I was there, I told lies about you. I said you were a horrible father. I need to go back and correct those lies. I need to make amends for the harm I have done. I want to let them know there is grace and forgiveness that I have never understood before."

I don't think we will ever fully understand God's grace this side of heaven, but when we experience it, we can stop lying to others and ourselves. We don't have to play the image game anymore. We don't have to be part of the clique, the crowd or the club. We don't have to apply religious cosmetics to make ourselves presentable to God. We just need to come home. We can accept our gifts, strengths, poverty and powerlessness. In Christ, we can be who we were created to be.

I love this prayer I heard years ago:

> *Lord, help me to understand what you had in mind*
> *when you made the original me.*

Once we experience the grace of God, we understand not just the "original us," but we can also finally be the original us. We can grieve our failures but never let them determine our life or destiny. We can let our heavenly Father take them and shape them into stepping-stones for His high calling in our life. We may be knocked down, beat up and counted nearly out, but we are never out of the game, because we are headed home.

Jesus said when you pray, understand how staggering the grace of God is toward you. You are praying to an incredibly giving heavenly Father who is waiting expectantly to bless you. He has sacrificed for you, because He is so affectionate and affirming toward you. In John 17 this is the Father Jesus prays you would come to know.

The Unconditional Love of Our Father

It is interesting to note that when the son finally gets home, even after the father runs out and greets him, the son starts his spiel. He has probably had weeks to practice it. He's been on the road a long time coming from the far country. He tells his father he has sinned and is sorry and not worthy to be called his son; he insists that he should be a slave instead. But as soon as the son tells the father he is sorry, the father is motioning to his servants to bring the robe, ring and sandals for his returning son. The son never gets to finish his spiel. The father never opens his mouth in response, because his actions are shouting his undying love for the boy. What a striking picture of our heavenly Father!

TWO THINGS WE WANT
TO HEAR FROM DAD

Through the years I have listened to literally thousands of men and women. At the center of so many hearts is a huge father wound, and there are two things these hurting people want to hear from their fathers.

I Believe in You

I would have given my right arm to hear a dad tell me that he believed in me. One of the deep grieving issues I had to face in life was the fact I would never hear those words from an earthly father. But my heavenly Father is saying that to me on a daily basis. In the Gospel of John, Jesus was saying, "When you think of your heavenly Father, think about a father who believes in you and loves to bless you. That is what I pray you come to understand" (see 17:23).

Please don't misunderstand me when I say I hear my heavenly Father tell me He believes in me on a daily basis. By faith I believe that is true, but I can have a great deal of difficulty hearing what He is saying to me at times. My wife and I had our first grandchild recently. Grandkids are incredible. I think they are God's reward for not killing your kids. And little Ashley is just like her mom in many ways. She loves for me to chase her, but she always wants to get caught. She loves it when we play "Got you." I am like that with God every now and then—pushing God's love away at times because I don't feel worthy of it but at the same time desperate for His affirmation.

One of these times, I was starting the day early with a counseling appointment. Seven o'clock in the morning is perhaps not the best time to hear people's deep and painful problems. But this particular day I was totally surprised. The young man said, "I don't have a problem we need to discuss, I just want to bless you this morning." I thought, *That is novel.* "Pastor, I want to wash your feet this morning," he continued. And I am thinking, *This is a cold, rainy Oregon morning and that doesn't sound appealing.* But he had already anticipated my hesitation, "I knew it would be cold, so I heated the water." I sat there feeling really uncomfortable as he washed my feet, and then I realized why. I wasn't in control. As a pastor you are in control because you are the one doing the giving. I could almost sense the Lord saying to me, "Ted, you can't control My love for you." Then my young foot-washing friend looked up at me and said, "Pastor Ted, I think the Lord has given me a word of encouragement for you." Now that kind of word I can receive.

My friend looked at me and continued, "I sense the Lord saying to you, 'When you were in the womb, I loved you. I saw your restrictions and how you fought to live and your warrior's heart touched My heart.'" I totally lost it. There is no way this young man could have known I was an illegitimate child and that my mother had wrapped her stomach so the pregnancy wouldn't show. Once again my heavenly Father leaned over and said, "Got you! I believe in you, son." You hang around with Father God long enough and you will start understanding His "got you's."

John 17:22 reads "I have given them the glory that you gave me, that they may be one as we are one." It is as if Jesus was saying, "I pray you would come to know you have a heavenly Father who is incredibly giving toward you." He will make sure you have what you need. He will protect you and guard you from the evil one. He waits expectantly for you to make the slightest move toward Him, so He can bless you. He is unbelievably compassionate, sacrificial, affectionate and affirming toward you. You are not defined by this world. You are your heavenly Father's kid.

I Am Sorry

The second thing so many men and women want to hear from their dad is "I am sorry"—not just for their father to admit he was wrong but also for them to freely admit to their father, "I am sorry too." There are no perfect earthly fathers or children. That is why every one of us needs to say to our dad or to our kids "I am sorry." Both sides always need to move toward each other.

> *The furious love of God is what makes it possible to become a pure-hearted disciple of Christ.*

With respect to our heavenly Father, His heart was wounded for us. That is how furious God's love is for us. That is why I came to deeply understand who I am and who I could be, as I discovered over and over again that the Father loves me. The furious love of God is what makes it possible for me to become a pure-hearted disciple of Christ. It is not about my faithfulness or my performance. I am counting on His love for me. An incredibly giving, patiently waiting, sacrificially pursuing, affectionate and affirming heavenly Father—His is the love I am counting on. A grace that I find truly amazing.

I am amazed not only by the grace that God has given me but also by His love in the lives of those I minister to. Once, a young lady stood before me following the fourth weekend service. She said, "Pastor Ted, I just love this place. I have fallen so in love with Jesus here. Would you pray for me?" I responded with a smile despite my deep fatigue, and said, "Sure, I would be delighted to pray for you. What do you need from God?" "Well, pastor, I am an exotic dancer. I have two small children; and as a single parent, it is tough to make ends meet. As a dancer I make a good income, yet after having said yes to Christ, I sense I need to seek another line of employment. I don't see any way I can do that. I need direction and probably a miracle from God."

She is not the only exotic dancer in the church. In fact, as I previously mentioned, we have had so many dancers start coming to East Hill that we had to start an alpha group just for them.[3] What brought tears to my eyes was the way in which she was standing there without shame—so obviously in love with Jesus, totally soaking in the grace of God. She truly felt the protecting and gracious presence of Christ. She was a vivid illustration of the fact that we essentially are only one request away from God's best in our lives. That week I had struggled as I dealt with all of the hassles and messes among believers. The petty arguments were unbelievable. The pressure of ministry literally had me feeling dry and crusty. I felt like that old sponge I had pulled out from under the kitchen sink. I wasn't carrying buckets of God's blessings; I was carrying a dusty, dry cup.

I almost asked this young lady to pray for me instead. I knew where the blessing was to be found—in the presence of our gracious heavenly Father. As I prayed, we both cried. Hers were tears of joy and mine were tears of relief from the weariness. But a giving, caring, sacrificial, affectionate and affirming heavenly Father knew exactly what we both needed.

God's grace is amazing, even when I get all turned around in ministry, when I am trying to serve Him and forget why. He will graciously send someone and remind me I am not the savior of the world—He is. And once again, I am surprised by another one of God's "got you's."

Let's look at how you are growing with respect to God the Father's amazing grace.

1.   How comfortable are you with calling God "Father"?

It's tough at times		I don't struggle with it		It deeply stirs me
1	2	3	4	5

2.   Do you see God as being very generous to you?

To be honest, not really		Sometimes		Incredibly so
1	2	3	4	5

3.   At times, do you feel like you are just surviving?

Yes, at times		I am doing okay		I am conquering my fears in Christ
1	2	3	4	5

4.   How comfortable are you with you?

I struggle at times		I feel okay		I am truly at peace with who I am in Christ
1	2	3	4	5

5. Did your father ever tell you that he believed in you?

		All the time; he was my main	
Never heard it	A couple of times	cheerleader	
1	2	3	4	5

Score _____ (Add together the numbers you circled.)

This score will be added to the results from chapter 7 and the total for Grace will be entered in the appropriate space on the Discipleship Development Analysis Tool in chapter 12.

CHAPTER SEVEN

IN HIS LOVING HANDS

The Shaping of the Potter's Wheel

My prayer is not that You pull them out of the world, but that You protect and guard them from the evil one. They are not defined by this world, just as I am not defined by this world or a part of it.
(SEE JOHN 17:15-16.)

When I served as a military flight instructor, I found that my most challenging task was to teach a young pilot air combat maneuvering (ACM), or dogfighting. The vast majority of students usually ended up with massive information overload in their initial flights. There was just too much happening too fast for them to keep up with the moment. I found that my ability to train them greatly improved once I realized there are very few students who are naturals in the cockpit. Therefore, I boiled ACM down to its bare essentials.

There were two simple maxims I told them they must never forget: Number one, never lose sight of the enemy, even if you have to break your neck to do it. And it can feel like that is happening when you are pulling a lot of Gs. Number two, learn to think in three dimensions of movement. We earthbound creatures essentially operate in two dimensions; but in a dogfight, you have to radically use the vertical to win.

In the spiritual battle we are involved in—called daily life—it is critical that we not focus on the enemy of our soul, but we must not lose sight of his actions against us. God's love for us is the vertical dimension that allows us to devastate the enemy, even against overwhelming odds. But we all have a problem—no one is natural in the Spirit. Paul stated it clearly:

> For all have sinned and fall short of the glory of God (Rom. 3:23).

That doesn't mean we are all involved in some horrible sin. Instead, we struggle with illusions that make our life crazy, like—one of my favorites—a propensity to get caught up in the "hurry up" disease. At times I find myself violently battling this malady.

I find myself sitting at a traffic signal, nervously waiting for the light to change. But I am so sick, I will automatically check out the make, model and year of the cars ahead of me as I pull up. I am checking them out, so I can anticipate which one will pull away fastest when the signal turns green. It gets worse. At the supermarket when I am waiting in line, I will instinctively pick out an individual in another line. Then I will compare how rapidly each of us moves through the checkout. If I get done before the person in the other line, I feel great. If I don't, then I feel frustrated. Now that is sick! In a way I'm kidding, but spiritually it definitely is a sign of problems within. You can never grow in your understanding of God's love for you *until you learn to wait on the Lord.*

THE MOST DIFFICULT LESSON OF ALL

Christ's prayer for us in John 17—regarding His grace—is an urgent one. In verse 15, He cries out that we would be protected from the evil one and in verse 16 points to the fact that we are not defined by this world. What defines us is the fact that God loves us as much as He loves Christ, which is the stunning statement of verse 23. Stop for a moment and let that truth grab you. It is simply incredible! I never would have believed such a thing if Christ hadn't said it. I know myself, and I am not that lovable. God's loving us this much is a difficult reality for us to grasp, because we tend to have such a shallow view of love. This tendency is why waiting and love—God's grace—are a difficult association for us to make in the unexpected changes of daily life.

God loves us as much as He loves Christ.

Understanding that association is one of the major differences between a man and a boy, or an adult and a child. I have counseled so many 40-, 50- and 60-year-old kids. Boys have to have everything right now—it doesn't matter if we are talking about sex, recognition or fulfillment in life—which is precisely why so many men end up being vulnerable to pornography, anger and a loss of integrity. They will never be men of God with any depth *until they learn to wait on the Lord.*

One of the major reasons spiritually mature believers learn to wait on the Lord is the nature of the problems they find themselves dealing with in life. You see, if we have a problem we can solve, we don't have a problem; instead, we have a decision about responsibility. What frequently brings us back to the Cross are all of the closed doors in life. When there is nowhere else to go, we have to wait on Him. But it is uniquely there where we catch a new glimpse—a new perspective of His astonishing love for us.

I only had been pastoring for about a year in the church I am now serving. Things were quite different in those days. The incurred indebtedness had buried the ministry; I was told my job was to go there and gracefully close the doors. But when I arrived, I realized the remaining people had such a heart for God. There was no way I could close the doors. Obviously, God had sent me there to turn things around. I took off like Indiana Jones *to save the day!* After a year, I had an emotional breakdown. I had never even experienced that in Vietnam. Of course, I was drunk all the time in 'Nam, but they frown on doing that if you are a pastor. One day I just fell apart—I couldn't walk or talk. All I could do was sit in my office and cry. Finally, I fell on my knees and listened to the Lord. As tears streamed down my face, the Lord asked me a simple question.

God never asks us questions because He needs information; He asks us questions so we can start thinking straight. "Ted, have you ever wondered why you end up here so frequently in your life?" "No, Lord, I never have." "Why is it you had to get a doctorate, not just a college degree? Yet everyone else in your family barely graduated from high school. And you couldn't just be a pilot; you had to be a Marine Corps fighter pilot. Why is it when someone from the squadron would fly under a bridge, the next day you would fly under it—upside down? Why do you do such things?" the Lord continued. "I don't know," I weakly replied. "Well, you'd better start finding out," the Holy Spirit lovingly challenged me. I later discovered I had essentially brought my dysfunctional family background and the Marine Corps into the ministry. That is why I had such a hard time understanding God's love in my life. Christ was graciously placing me on the potter's wheel of His divine purposes.

THE POTTER'S WHEEL OF LIFE

Finding yourself on the potter's wheel is not a novel life experience. The prophet Jeremiah's struggle is a classic example of how confusing things can get at times as we follow the Lord. Jeremiah is facing opposition from nearly everyone, including his own family, as he attempts to obey God. The Lord essentially says, "Jerry, you need to go down to the potter's house" (see Jer. 18:1-2). If you have a heart for God, you too will end up down at the potter's house. And God usually calls us to wait on Him when we are the least likely to do so.

I was busy pastoring a challenging situation and the last thing I needed to do was wait on the Lord. I needed to keep things going. I had to pull through this thing! But as I lay facedown on the floor of my office, it finally dawned on me: Maybe trying harder wasn't the answer. At the end of all of our struggles, we are brought to the place of being face-to-face with God.

Jeremiah was in a far worse situation. The Israelites were trying to kill him for speaking God's word, and even his family was part of the necktie party. That is why he finally admitted: "God, I don't know what in the world You are doing in my life. I mean, what is up with You? You didn't do what I thought You were going to do" (see Jer. 18:19-23).

God's Grace Doesn't End Here

God reached down to a man who was emotionally wounding his wife. He reached down to a man who was an alcoholic and a sex addict. He reached down to a man caught in the insanity of the Vietnam War. And He didn't just reach down once. He has kept reaching out to me, speaking to me when I didn't have a clue what a great gift my wife and kids were to me. When you really have been in the mud, you are just glad He picked you up. Christ has repeatedly declared to me things in life that would hold me down and destroy me. I can imagine God saying, "Let him loose. I am putting him on the sovereign wheel of My divine purposes. I am going to show him just how deep My love for him goes."

When you are in the midst of the shaping process—and all of us are at times—the experience can become rather intense. We cry out, "Oh, Lord, fix this. Straighten this out or take it away. Lord, I am going in circles and can't figure out what is going on!" And the Lord will give us this amazing response—no. The reason for His seemingly uncaring response is that He is using the situation to heal or strengthen us. We may be in the midst of a storm so that we can learn to trust Him.

The New Testament uses the word "test" in a unique way with respect to God and his kids (see 1 Tim. 3:10; Heb. 11:17; 1 Pet. 1:7). God tests us, but it is never a destructive testing. He doesn't pull us off the assembly line and then smash us with a hammer to see if we pass the test. He already knows what is within us. He brings us to a time of testing so that *we know what is within us—so we realize we can pass the test! God designs the test so that we can win!*

When everything is spinning and a blur, it doesn't seem to make much sense. That is how I felt as I lay facedown on the carpet in my office listening to God. It seemed like before I straightened one thing out, here came something else! It seemed as if it was never going to stop. However, that day I saw something with the eyes of my heart I will never forget. I realized that the feet spinning the wheel of my circumstances had been *scarred by nails*.

Obviously, during Jeremiah's time, electrical power had not been invented yet. The potter would form the vessel on a spinning wheel, which he propelled with his feet using a counterbalancing wheel underneath. I came to understand as never before that God not only had His hand on my life, but He also had His foot on the wheel of my circumstances. Hell doesn't control the spin of my life. If it did, I would have been thrown by my life's difficulties years ago. I would have been beaten to death by one of my stepfathers, caught a bullet in combat or eventually destroyed my life with alcohol. God also has His foot on your circumstances and situations. He knows precisely how fast to spin you.

God's Love Is a Wake-Up Call

David cried out in the Psalms: "My times are in your hands" (Ps. 31:15). He was declaring the fact that God was closely monitoring his situation, even though circumstances weren't going his way. A crazed King Saul was trying to turn David into a kabob with his spear, even though he had done nothing wrong.

Our struggles usually are not that intense. We can miss what God is up to in our lives, because we are numbed by routine. You know the scene. The guy gets up at the same old time every morning. He walks into the same old bathroom and looks at the same old face in the same old mirror. Then he walks into the same old kitchen and gets the same old cereal bowl. He eats the same old breakfast, drinks the same old coffee and kisses the same old wife. Then he goes to the same old job. He does the same old job in the same old way and listens to the same old boss tell the same old jokes. Then he comes home the same old way, has the same old dinner and, in our part of the country, watches the same old Lakers basketball team beat the same old Blazers. He falls asleep watching the same old TV and eventually gets up and goes to the same old bed. Then he asks the same old wife the same old question—and gets the same old answer. He rolls over and sets the same old alarm clock to get up and do the same old thing all over again. It's nuts!

My friend, have you ever turned and really looked at your mate after you have been married a while? At times I have turned and looked at Diane as she is beside me in bed, or on a Monday morning when we have breakfast together, and I have been overwhelmed by my intense love for her. Suddenly, the past 34 years together come back like a flood—the laughter, the tears, the highs, the lows, the personal jokes and nick-names we share in common—and all run before my mind in rapid review. I am struck by all those moments, memories and victories we shared together. I am treasuring those things as one who has been deeply loved, and I will carry them with me to the grave.

Recently such a precious moment hit me upside the heart. As I sat there thinking of what my life would be like without my wife—how empty it would be—I started tearing up. I wasn't cry-ing. My eyes have just been sweating a lot since I came to Christ. As I was watching my wife, Christ was watching me. He wasn't evaluating me. Instead, He was saying things like, "Ted, I love you far more than you love your wife. That love you feel now for Diane is just a little gift from Me, to remind you of how deep My love for you really is." You may be like me. You may be like David. You may never have had a physical father who loved you, but you have a heavenly Father who loves you every moment of your life. That is why you can develop the skill of waiting on Him, even when your world is whirling.

A SOVEREIGN SHAPING PROCESS

God's foot is truly on the difficult circumstances of your life. He is graciously sovereign in your life. Some might say, "Wait a minute, if God is absolutely sovereign in my life, that must mean I don't have any choices in life. Where does my free will come into play?" There is a very clear answer to those questions: God is absolutely sovereign and at the same time you have a free will. What? How can that be?

I remember one of the questions asked of me during the oral portion of my doctoral examination. My thesis dealt with the astrophysics and theology of Genesis chapters 1 and 2. Not many of the examiners on the review panel had an extensive background in the area of cosmology, so they quickly turned to classic theological questions. One professor asked me, "Mr. Roberts, what do you do with the sovereignty of God and the free will of man?" I just smiled and simply said, "Well, sir, I preach the sovereignty of God on Sunday morning and the free will of man on Sunday night." They all laughed and understood what I was saying.

At the core of every great truth in the Christian faith lies a mystery. The divinity of Christ and the humanity of Christ go beyond the human mind's ability to comprehend. So do the concept of the Trinity and the question of God's sovereignty and man's free will. Many philosophers and theologians have tried to explain these mysteries. Augustine, the towering theologian of the Early Church, commented that great theologies will always lead you to one thing—worship.[1]

That is a marvelous way to describe our struggle. Once we truly come to grips with what God has to say in His Word with respect to who He is and who we are, we only have one option: Fall to our knees and admit we don't fully understand Him. Although we don't understand with our heads, our hearts rejoice in the reality of the truth, which is why we burst forth in praise to our magnificent God.

Recent scientific study into the nature of our cosmos seems to indicate our universe began with at least 10 dimensions of reality, but soon collapsed into the four dimensions we are familiar with.[2] Try for a moment to comprehend a being who exists in at least six additional dimensions of reality beyond our paltry four.

The shaping process of the potter's wheel almost always goes against your background and defined comfort zones. Everything within you feels like jumping off the wheel. Yet you stay on the wheel. Why is that? Because at some point we find ourselves in the same situation Peter faced in John 6 when everyone was leaving. Jesus had just made one of the most startling statements in the New Testament:

I tell you the truth, unless you eat the flesh of the Son of Man and drink his blood, you have no life in you (John 6:53).

In verse 64, John tells us Jesus knew from the beginning who did not believe in Him. Apparently, He was raising the cost of being a disciple, because such a statement would definitely drop His rating with the Pharisees. People who were not willing to go against popular opinion were getting off the wheel in droves. Jesus asked Peter if he was getting off the wheel as well. A confused, bewildered and befuddled Simon simply said, "Lord, to whom shall we go? You have the words of eternal life" (John 6:68). In other words: Jesus, You have touched my life and I could never go back to what I did before.

Diane was putting our newborn daughter to sleep, and I was outside looking up into the beautiful Texas sky. I was watching the military aircraft fly overhead and I thought of all the night instrument training missions I had flown. We had just sold nearly everything we had and were heading to seminary. I had resigned my commission as a Marine Corps flight officer, a career achievement I had dreamed about and worked for since I was five years old. As I stood out there in the midst of those whirling circumstances, I thought, *Have you totally lost your mind? You should be flying planes, not becoming some preacher.* But I couldn't go back. I couldn't climb off the potter's wheel of the Lord's plan for my life. Oh, sure, it would have been physically possible to step off the wheel. It wasn't because I was such a strong and virtuous person; it was simply because He touched me.

We are involved in this rather unique spiritual fight in our life. The enemy isn't fighting with us so much over who we are right now; rather, he is resisting us tooth and nail over who we will be once God gets finished with us. And somehow we sense it within. Maybe we sense it from God the Father's expression as He looks upon us. He is never discouraged with the reality He sees in our lives. He instead is constantly mindful of a higher reality. This doesn't make a lot of sense to us, and in the battle we can become confused because we are so prone to focus on what we need right now. Yet God doesn't seem to care, because all the while He is talking to us about where we will be. That is precisely why learning to listen to Him is such a foundational skill in learning how to walk in His love.

THE DEEP DILEMMA

The reader is faced with a deep dilemma—the vessel of clay has been marred in the potter's hands. It is a dilemma because if it had fallen out of the hands of the potter, we could understand. Or if it had jumped off the wheel, we could understand. This is not just a theological dilemma; it is a profoundly personal issue. You can be in the hands of a sovereign, gracious God, yet find yourself marred. But the divine potter never slips—He is never the cause of the problem. That is one of the few givens or

> *The enemy isn't fighting with us so much over who we are right now; rather, he is resisting us tooth and nail over who we will be once God gets finished with us.*

absolutes in life. It is one truth you can totally count on. The problem is the clay He is working with. In the process of shaping, at times imperfections will appear. Such imperfections will be revealed in our lives. And who can use a marred vessel? What good is it? It seems the potter's purpose has been destroyed by the weakness of the material He is working with. Whatever you put in the vessel will leak out.

Ask God to Fill Your Leaks
Jeremiah was leaking like a sieve with respect to his anger toward God. And the harder God pressed him, the more his marred nature rose to the surface. In chapter 20, Jeremiah accuses God of lying to him and calls Him every name a prophet of God could use (see vv. 7-8). Yet if he tries to just keep his mouth shut and forget God, he can't. He declares, "His word is in my heart like a fire, a fire shut up in my bones" (Jer. 20:9).

When I came to Christ, I gladly hopped on the wheel of God's shaping process. But soon the spinning and shaping work of the Lord became overwhelming. I was angry a lot. In fact, it seemed the harder I tried the angrier I became. I would make arrogant comments that seemed to come from the very depths of my soul.

Years later Diane would tell me how deeply I had embarrassed her with my public comments. Of course, fighter pilots are not known for their humility. It seemed as if the imperfections were only getting worse with each additional touch of God in my life. I wanted off the wheel. I couldn't handle all this spiritual stuff. My life was a lot more manageable before I came to Christ. Yet I couldn't let go, because He had such a deep hold on my heart.

One day Diane suggested we go and visit a Teen Challenge ministry. It had recently started in a city near the air base where we were stationed. I had kind of given up on church, yet deep within my heart I hungered for God. So when the suggestion came up I thought, *Why not?* The founder of Teen Challenge had written a book that touched my heart and helped me make a commitment to Christ. I will never forget the scene I encountered at Teen Challenge. It was a street ministry, so it didn't fit the military criteria of having it "all squared away." There were folks with hair hanging down to their knees—this was in the '70s—and there I stood with a billiard-ball haircut. (In those days, I polished my head as well as my shoes.) I was a career Marine Corps officer who quickly realized these people obviously hadn't got with the program. No one seemed to have the slightest idea what they were doing. They were just hanging out and talking about Jesus. My wife loved it; she was having a ball. Soon I noticed she was missing. Somehow in this crowd of people I had managed to lose my wife. I asked an individual who was passing out coffee, "Do you know where my wife went?" "Sure, she is being prayed for in the back room." I eventually found her.

It was total mayhem. People were praying for her with their hands in the air, speaking with all kinds of strange sounding words. I asked an individual what was going on. "She told us she wanted a touch from God, so we are praying for her to be filled with the Holy Spirit. Do you want a touch from God? Do you want to be filled with the Holy Spirit as well?" Something within tugged at my heart, yet at the same time I was not going to let these strange-looking people mess with my wife.

"Sure," I fired back, "Jesus, fill me with the Holy Spirit I pray. Now, I am taking my wife out of here. Do you understand?" "Okay, dude. Whatever," he said, as he backed away from me. I grabbed Diane and headed for the car. I had had just about enough of this place. As I briskly walked along, I told her I would never go to such a nuthouse again. She nodded her head in agreement but had this silly, wide grin on her face.

As things turned out, we served for over a year as elders and mentors in that ministry. I spent numerous hours talking with and counseling kids who were on drugs or in trouble. How I ended up serving those kids came from a significant moment of waiting in my life.

Recognize When God Fills Your Leaks

I was in a ferocious hurry. I had been scheduled as the trainer for three flights, and by the time you add up briefings, debriefings and flight delays, I knew the day was going to be a pressure cooker. By the third flight I was fit to be tied. It was a flight to train young pilots in the fine art of bombing, which involves a lot more than launching a little practice bomb through the air. It involves the takeoff, coordination and oversight of four aircraft, three student pilots and the trainer. You have specific times you have to arrive over the practice range, which means a great deal of things can go wrong. The captain immediately caught my attention. He was a total mess. The plane was a mess; it obviously hadn't been prepared correctly for takeoff. And the captain didn't bow and scrape before me—he clearly didn't appreciate my station in life. I mentally took note of his name and logged it in my memory, so I could write him up once I returned from the flight.

He also didn't help me strap into the aircraft, which makes things rather difficult. You almost have to be double-jointed to get everything hooked up correctly without assistance. I was furious by that point. Finally, I managed to get strapped in and start the engine. I found myself further behind schedule. As I went through the preflight checks, the captain appeared on the right side of the aircraft to give me the thumbs-up sign that takeoff trim was set and nothing was leaking from the aircraft. As I cycled the controls to make sure nothing was restricting their movement, he gave me another thumbs-up.

It was then that God showed up. It was then that God touched my life. As I looked at the captain, suddenly from my innermost being came this flow of love. I suddenly saw the young man in a totally different light. I could clearly see how arrogant and domineering I had been and how afraid he was. I saw the scene as God saw it. This wasn't just some warm fuzzy feeling. This was a God kind of love welling up in my soul.

Suddenly, I was on the verge of tears. Then I was crying! I initially couldn't understand what was happening to me. I dropped down the visor on my helmet as the tears started. *Maybe I am having a delayed stress reaction from Vietnam*, I thought. Then I realized how foolish that assessment was. I was weeping over the arrogance and sinfulness of my heart and, at the same time, weeping over God's compassion for this 19-year-old kid on the flight line who had to put up with me. I also was weeping for the joy of God's touch on my life. Then the Lord reminded me of what had happened the night before, *You asked Me to fill you with the Holy Spirit, didn't you? Well, I did.* As a marred vessel in the hands of God, I had received the Holy Spirit when I said yes to Christ in a Vietnam bunker. Yet I still leaked a lot, and I was spiritually drying up.

Peter made a critical observation concerning all our lives. A heated debate was going on in the Church at the time. The question was whether or not Gentiles should be admitted into the Church. It seems like a ridiculous question today, but the reason it is so obvious to us today is because of what Peter pointed out to the leaders of the Church in Jerusalem:

> God, who knows the heart, showed that he accepted them [the Gentiles] by giving the Holy Spirit to them, just as he did to us. He made no distinction between us and them, for he purified their hearts by faith (Acts 15:8-9).

Peter is saying that on the Day of Pentecost not only did supernatural things happen in our lives, but we also spoke in a supernatural language. There was a fire at work in each of our hearts, cleansing us. Peter was careful in his choice of words. "Purified their hearts" comes from the word *katharos*, which means "to clean off, to cleanse from filth."[3] Now that doesn't mean the individual is cleansed forever, never to sin again. Peter would find himself in the days ahead frequently cleaning mud off his face from having put one or the other of his sandals in his mouth. He is the one disciple that gives me tremendous hope for my life.

That day in the cockpit, as I cried my eyes out, God took the marred vessel of my life and washed it once again from the inside out. In this fallen world we need this cleansing flow on a regular basis. That is why it is so important for us to learn the art and discipline of waiting on the Lord. I could have just pushed through those feelings and told myself to snap out of it, only to miss a moment that, frankly, changed my life.

> *In waiting before the Lord, we begin to grasp His love for us and take it to a whole new depth.*

FINAL THOUGHTS

We tend to view waiting on the Lord as a time of inactivity, but so frequently it is a time of slowing down enough to finally see things from God's perspective. When we slow down, our efforts become more fruitful. In waiting before the Lord, we come face-to-face with the fact we are in His hands; we begin to grasp His love for us and take it to a whole new depth. A lack of patience isn't really a problem as we learn to simply sit and wait; instead, it is a challenge to learn about God's love for us in a deeper way. It is such a powerful weapon against hell. The next time hell tries to talk to you about your flaws and failures, you just remind it that you are still in God's hands. And by the time Christ finishes His work in you, hell is going to be in serious trouble!

Let's look at the issue of your being in God's loving and gracious hands. Read each question or statement and circle the number that best corresponds to your answer.

1. I struggle with always feeling like I am in a hurry in my life.

Yes, I often rush from one thing to another		Occasionally		I am at peace in my hectic world
1	2	3	4	5

2. When your world is spinning and feels out of control, what are your first thoughts?

God, have You deserted me?		God, are You there?		God, what are You teaching me?
1	2	3	4	5

3. How hard is it for you to deeply listen to God in really difficult times?

A real struggle		Not too difficult		Not hard at all; it is my first response
1	2	3	4	5

4. How long has it been since you were simply overwhelmed and brought to a point of worship by the awesomeness of God?

Frankly, I never have		It's been awhile		It's a frequent occurrence
1	2	3	4	5

5. How easy is it for you to recognize the marred areas in the vessel of your life?

I struggle with what they are		I have my blind spots		I know them well
1	2	3	4	5

Score _____ (Add together the numbers you circled.)
Enter score from chapter 6 _____
Total score _____ (Add together the scores from chapters 6 and 7.)

Take this total score for Grace and enter it in the appropriate space on the Discipleship Development Analysis Tool in chapter 12.

CHAPTER EIGHT

WHAT DO YOU DO WHEN YOU DON'T KNOW WHAT TO DO?

Traversing the Valley of Dry Bones

Make [put your name here] *holy, purify and heal and make* [put your name here] *wholly yours by means of the truth. Your Word is the consecrating and healing truth.*

(*SEE JOHN 17:17.*)

While on the Internet, I immediately caught sight of an article from the *Meridian Star* newspaper. I was stationed just outside Meridian, Mississippi, for basic jet training, so this got my attention. The article read as follows:

> George Phillips of Meridian was going to bed when his wife told him he'd left the light on in the garden shed, which she could see from the bedroom window. George opened the back door to go turn off the light, but saw people in the shed stealing things. He phoned the police, who asked, "Is someone in your house?" And George said, "No." They informed Mr. Phillips all patrols were busy and he should simply lock his door. An officer would be along when available. George said, "Okay," hung up and counted to 30 and phoned the police again.
>
> "Hello, I just called you a few seconds ago because there were people in my shed. You don't have to worry about them now, because I've just shot them all." He hung up.
>
> Within five minutes, three police cars, an armed response unit and an ambulance showed up at the Phillips's residence. Of course, the police caught the burglars red-handed. One policeman said to George, "I thought you said you'd shot them all!" George said, "I thought you said there was nobody available!"[1]

What do you do if you can't figure out how to get the "cops" to show up in your life? What do you do when you don't know what to do, when you can't figure out what to do financially, or you don't have a clue how to turn your marriage around? Maybe you find yourself beside the hospital bed of a friend or relative and the news isn't good. What do you do? Crises are when the real depth of discipleship is determined. Discipleship is forged in the fiery times, not the easy times. Even as Christ prayed in the Upper Room, His soul was struggling with what to do (see John 17:11). The battle would come to an agonizing climax in the Garden of Gethsemane. When Jesus uttered the words in the Upper Room, "Sanctify them by the truth; your word is truth" (John 17:17), He expressed them in the truculent turmoil of personal battle. But this is not an unusual experience. Christ is simply walking in the well-worn footprints of everyone who decides to passionately follow the heavenly Father. Of course, He did it uniquely without sin. We all have to decide what is true in the tough times of life—our worries or the Word of God.

Discipleship is forged in the fiery times of crisis, not the easy times.

NEVER ALONE IN THE VALLEY

A classic picture of the struggle every passionate-hearted disciple will have with God is found in Ezekiel. It is one of the most challenging books in the Old Testament. A rabbi in the Middle Ages wouldn't allow a young man to study two particular books of the Bible in depth until he was 30 years of age. The Song of Songs was one, because the language is too sexual. It is hot stuff! And the other was the book of Ezekiel, because it seems to be pretty strange stuff.[2]

There are two chapters in the book of Ezekiel most folks are somewhat familiar with. Chapter 1 is a section I like to call the crop-circle chapter. Chapter 37 could be called the anklebone chapter. A number of people have read chapter 1 and think it is rather weird, given all the gleaming wheels. In Ezekiel wheels fly around with rims full of eyes, and some folks conclude, "UFOs right there in the Bible!" There is a much more reasonable answer than crop circles: simply believe what Ezekiel has to say.

In 597 B.C., when Ezekiel was approximately 25 years of age, the Babylonian army devastated Jerusalem. The Temple was destroyed and Ezekiel's hopes of ever serving as a priest were forever dashed. Five years later, he reached the age when he could have served as a priest, but instead he was breaking up rock on a Babylonian chain gang. He is far from his homeland—his Temple and its worship a dim memory. As he scans the searing hot plains, he notices a thunderstorm building in the mountains to the north. Here is a graphic picture of a man who doesn't know where God is headed in his life.

Chapter 1 becomes a transcendent description of an awesome and indescribable encounter with the person and power of God. As the storm passes, the rain glistens on Ezekiel's forehead, and he falls facedown as he hears his heavenly Father speaking to his soul. Father God calls him to be a priest and prophet in God's throne room in the midst of captivity. Ezekiel falls before the mighty love of Father God as Moses did at the burning bush, as Joshua did in the wilderness outside Jericho, as Daniel did in his captivity, as Paul did in his prison cell and as John did on Patmos—his island of captivity.

In every case, God the Father knew exactly where they were, despite the ropes of their reality that seemed to hem them in and even in their struggle of trying to figure out what to do. God spoke His word of promise to them, a word that not only transformed their situation but also touched and changed them as well.

In chapter 37, the anklebone, the greatest miracles take

place. It is one thing to see the Red Sea part, but it is another thing entirely to see the walls of cynicism, bitterness and hopelessness be parted in people's hearts. That is the greatest miracle of all. Look at how God challenges Ezekiel:

> The hand of the LORD was upon me, and He brought me out by the Spirit of the LORD and set me in the middle of a valley; it was full of bones. He asked me, "Son of man, can these bones live?" I said, "O Sovereign LORD, you alone know." Then He said to me, "Prophesy to these bones and say to them, 'Dry bones, hear the word of the LORD! This is what the Sovereign LORD says to these bones: I will make breath enter you, and you will come to life. I will attach tendons to you and make flesh come upon you and cover you with skin; I will put breath in you, and you will come to life. Then you will know that I am the LORD'" (Ezek. 37:1,3-6).

The amazing power of that promise given to Ezekiel was that Israel, symbolized by the dry bones, not only survived captivity, but she also thrived. And in many ways, it was because of Ezekiel's ministry. Human history shows *no other* example of a captive nation that not only managed to keep its culture intact but also returned to its native land. Not only did the people return to Israel, but God also healed the nation of rampant idolatry. Israel from this point on became a staunch monotheistic people. And God didn't rescue Israel just once in her history but twice! In 1948, the Jewish people once again returned to the Promised Land after years of captivity.

Now all of this makes you suspect that *nothing, absolutely nothing, can stand in the way of a Word-believing follower of the Lord!* It doesn't matter how many times you go down. It doesn't matter how many times you have been counted out. You will never stay down, because God's Word within you will lift you back up.

You will never stay down, because God's Word within you will lift you back up.

DOWN IN THE VALLEY

There is no avoiding it. If we faithfully follow Father God, we will at times find ourselves in the valley, as Ezekiel did. When God grabs a hold of our life, we don't get to pick where He takes us. Recognizing the importance of Ezekiel's situation shows us that just the presence of the power is not enough at times. Without God's Word to him, Ezekiel could never have pulled things together.

Ever been in the valley of dry bones? Tossing and turning at two o'clock in the morning—wrestling with impossible situations and looking at your finances, marriage, family and body. There appears to be no way things can turn around and come together. Can these bones really live? Ezekiel's response is usually our response: "I don't know. I don't know what to do! I can't pull all of this stuff together. I have all these problems, dilemmas and difficulties. I don't know if this will work." Yet it wasn't Ezekiel's overwhelming faith that released the miracle; it wasn't his confidence in his call, character or capabilities. However, things turned around.

How? Ezekiel did something so simple yet so profound that many folks miss it as they read the familiar passage—chapter 37. He spoke the promise God had given him. He stepped outside of his difficulty and started speaking to it. He stopped talking about the problem and started talking about God's promise. Now he wasn't just flipping through the Old Testament trying to find a promise from God; rather, he spoke what God had spoken to him. Over the years this passage has convinced me that there are two actions that can really turn things around in my life.

Journaling in the Valley
The first is what I call biblical journaling. Many individuals have developed the habit of journaling—writing out their prayers to the Lord and then praying them. That was helpful for a period of time in my life, but I desired more. I needed to get to the deepest emotions of my soul. I wanted something that would reach all the way down into my spirit. That was when I began having an ongoing dialogue with the Word of God. I have found it to be absolutely life changing. Paul tells us to take up the "sword of the Spirit, which is the word of God" (Eph. 6:17). I use the acrostic SWORD to create my dialogue.

S—Find the Scripture for the day in whatever systematic plan you are using to read through the Bible in a year. There are many plans available; simply select one that works best for you.

W—Welcome the Holy Spirit's guidance to teach you, to reveal things from God's Word you haven't seen before, not in the sense of new revelation, but practical application. Especially invite Him to speak to the deepest needs of your heart, because frequently people are concerned about the symptoms in life and miss the core issues.

O—Observe with pen in hand, literally. Write out what the Lord is speaking to *you* from His Word. I get a little nervous when someone is getting a "word from the Lord" out of thin air. Yes, the Lord desires to speak to you personally, but be cautious not to call something a word from God when it's nothing more than an upset stomach. There is nothing like the Holy Spirit supernaturally underlining a verse or passage to your heart from the Word. One word from God is worth more than a billion words from man.

R—Rejoice. Give God thanks for speaking to you. When I do this, there usually is a further release of His heart to me. The depth of my intimacy and communication with Him only increases. The Word begins to grow within me. It becomes something personal and passionate between the Holy Spirit and myself. To this day there are passages that every time I read them I still remember hearing the Lord whisper to me of His love and grace. They have become part of His ongoing love letter to me.

D—Decide what you are going to do in response to the truth God has spoken to you. Get yourself a notebook and begin to write down your responses to the Word you have received. Generally the responses fall into three categories.

1. *Precious truths.* These are insights that not only are applicable to your life but also are useful to share with others in a Bible study, accountability group or in a teaching format. Some of the most tender insights God will give you are to be shared with others, not as preaching bullets, but as words of encouragement to weary and struggling hearts.

2. *Promises.* These are the words that become like beacons in those times when you don't know what to do. It is as if you are on a stormy sea at night trying to get to a safe harbor, and these promises become shining beacons directing your soul to safety. God hasn't changed His promises to you no matter how much water you may be taking on. Jesus is in your

boat, and that means you're not going down!

3. *Principles.* These are the lessons learned—usually the hard way! In the midst of life's tough times, when things are falling apart, God will graciously lean over and instruct you through His Word. Perhaps His instruction explains what you should have done or why people reacted the way they did. Sometimes it's just plain old sin you didn't realize at the time, but now His Word makes it clear to you. I have learned if I don't write down the painful lessons I have experienced, I usually will have to learn them all over again. Over the years as you read and reread the lessons learned, you will begin to notice a pattern in your blunders, which is why the Holy Spirit will underline various themes in your Scripture reading. With practice, your weaknesses can become the very strengths through which God displays His glory.

Be sure to write out in prayer form what you are going to do about the precious truths, promises and principles you have received from God. Revelation without response leads to boredom or, worse yet, religious voyeurism.

Speaking in the Valley

The second part of seeing things turned around in my life flows naturally from the first. It flows naturally in the spirit but not in the flesh. In other words, it takes some good old-fashioned guts to trust in God's promises and do what Ezekiel did.

During one of our midweek services, I asked a young man who had recently become part of our flock to share his story of how he ended up at East Hill Church. Here is what he had to say:

In early March, with $200 in my pocket, I set out to execute my plan. I was going to leave a suicide note, eat a meal and then go out in the woods and blow my brains out. When I left the restaurant, instead of driving my car out to the woods, God guided my car to the parking lot of East Hill Church. I ended up sitting outside the big glass doors of the church at one o'clock in the morning. Confused, cold and scared, I asked God to give me a sign. I still was convinced He didn't love me; I would be better off dead. After an hour, a man came out of nowhere. (He was part of the maintenance crew at East Hills.) He asked if I was okay. I told him that I was hurting and trying to find some healing. He replied, "You are in the right place." After some small talk, he went on his way. He had no idea what my intentions were. About 15 minutes later, he came back and said, "God wants me to tell you something: Don't do what you are going to do. He loves you."

I broke down and started crying and told him my whole story. He told me about God's awesome love and the plans He had for my life. He prayed over me with God feeding him the words I needed to hear. I went home, disassembled the 12-gauge shotgun, and the next week I came back to East Hill and accepted Jesus Christ into my life.

After 23 years of drug abuse, a marriage of 19 years that had finally disintegrated and a 12-gauge shotgun to his head, my friend turned around. He was able to do that because of the word that God the Holy Spirit spoke through an obedient disciple of Christ that night—a word that had the power to bring the dry bones of his life back together. Since that night he has put his shotgun away and picked up the sword of the Spirit, becoming a uniquely powerful warrior for the Lord.

THE DEEPEST VALLEY

One of the things that has taken me a long time to understand is that all of God's truth is relational—it is understood in community. Even God Himself is only understood in community— God the Father, God the Son and God the Holy Spirit. For years I had been trained that if you couldn't see something on a set of charts or a computer flight data readout, then it wasn't real or important. However, the deeper things of life—biblical truths— are only understood relationally, not just rationally.

That is why one of the greatest obstacles to my trusting in God's Word was my lack of trust in Him personally. It showed up in the symptoms of my relentless drive to be okay. In a frantic attempt to silence the inner voices of not being good enough, I was driven in sports, in academics and in the military. The problem was that those pursuits gave me awards for being driven, so I never got down to the core of the problem. I was receiving all these pats on the back, but there still was this yawning chasm in my soul.

As with many people, the core of my problem was found in the past. I was convinced my Mom deeply loved me, but the message got confused You see, my single-parent mother fought a losing battle with alcoholism. One night, Mom told me she would only be a minute, as she headed into a bar to meet a friend. Several hours later I started rummaging through the glove compartment of the car and found some razor blades. As a five-year-old, I had never seen razor blades before. And in those days, they wrapped each blade individually in some interesting colored paper. The results were inevitable. Soon the front seat of the car was covered with blood. A police officer just happened to show up, wondering what a little guy was doing alone in a parked car at one o'clock in the morning. He bandaged me up and went in and dragged Mom out of the bar. In my eyes, I had failed Mom and messed up the car. Needless to say, she wasn't happy about the whole thing and she let me know just how upset she was.

It took me years to figure out it was the booze talking to me that night, not the heart of my mother. Years later I learned Mom had been thrown down a well when she was about five because her Mom didn't want her. When I discovered that part of her background, the anger and shame of the razor-blade incident faded like a morning mist before the brightness of the rising sun. As an adult, I had the delight of leading Mom to Christ, and I will always remember the look of joy and pride in her eyes as she sat in the second row in the first church I ever pastored—*taking notes!* Now Mom never took notes on anything; but if her boy was speaking, it was a different matter.

My point in all of this is when we are embedded in and constantly battling our real or imagined past failings, we are fighting a losing battle. We will end up saying to ourselves, in one way or another, *I don't really trust in the love of God,* which means no matter how deeply we agree with the Word of God, when push comes to shove, we will not trust in it. Therefore, at some point in our lives, we will end up in a valley of dry bones—feeling disconnected and alone.

Preoccupation with past wounds, present weaknesses or character defects eventually directs our emotions in self-destructive ways. We end up in a valley of selfishness. Denial, blame and anger directed toward someone else become the dry bones we end up living with on a daily basis. I can tell you from personal experience that the language we speak to ourselves in that valley is harsh, abusive and faultfinding. It is abusive with respect to others and ourselves. Rather than being delighted with anything good inside, we become shocked and frustrated no matter how small the failure, which means there is no possibility of long-term inner peace. However, once I started tentatively relating to Christ and allowing His grace to sink deep within me, I was shocked. I was appalled at the way in which I had judged myself. I would never have judged anyone else with the ruthlessness to which I was constantly subjected myself.

When you've been a counselor as long as I have, you realize a lot of folks try to hide their true selves from God. Now it seems ridiculous to try and hide from God, but we learned it from our great-great-great-great-great-great-great (and *many* more greats) . . . granddad, Adam. We try to hide, because we simply don't trust God to be able to handle all that goes on in our heads and hearts. Can Jesus accept our horrible thoughts, our selfish fantasies, our bizarre dreams and our embarrassing sexual temptations? We instinctively don't feel that He can, because others can't. So we withhold from Jesus what is most needed for our deepest healing. We may believe what God says is true, but we can't come to really trust Him. And that is when discipleship becomes a head game rather than a heart-transforming journey. We know the facts but can't take the steps or speak His promises with conviction, despite the valley we are facing.

Here is one of the most important foundational facts you have to grasp if you are ever going to become a pure-hearted disciple of Christ: God perceives you in a radically different way from the way you tend to perceive yourself. *God the Father is constantly seeing you through His eyes of grace.*

I was working out at the gym and having a good day with the free weights when this young buck pulled up beside me—an earring in each ear, a do-rag on his head and his Walkman set at concussion level. He looked over at me as I was doing a set of curls and said, "How old are you, dude?" I responded by telling him my age—minus a few years, of course. "Wow, for an old guy you are really cool," he said in amazement. Sometimes God can encourage you through the most unusual sources!

However, most of us have an extremely difficult time hearing God's words of grace and encouragement to us. Later that same week I met another do-rag young man when he ambled up to me after I spoke at a men's conference—his huge frame obviously very familiar with weight lifting. His enormous hand enveloped mine as he smiled from ear to ear and declared, "Ted, you rock!" Soon the smile faded and he said, "I once was very close to God but things have faded. I wonder if I even trust Christ anymore. I seem to keep on doing the same destructive things with women; but I can't get off the treadmill. I wish I were closer to Christ. What you said touched my heart."

Later at that same conference a pastor confided in me. "Ted, I once had a fire that burned for Christ deep inside of me. Yet the constant pressures and criticisms of pastoring have extinguished the flame within." Tears came to his eyes as he paused and said, "As you spoke of Father God, I cried. I wish I could have the relationship I once had with the Father. I am having all kinds of sexual temptations going on in my head."

I want you to do something with me right now. Ask yourself, *How is God the Father going to respond to these two guys?* This is not some New Age exercise. I'm not saying you are God, so relax! But how do you see the Father responding to these men? Would God still see them as having a relationship with Him? Would He see them as loving Him? What would be His response to them? Unfortunately, for a lot of church folks, they would see these men as being out of fellowship with God.

I swept both these men up in my arms and wept with them.

I loved them. I think most folks would do exactly the same. They would embrace these men—not with an "appropriate" Christian hug but with a deep sense of compassion. As I hugged one of the men and wept with him, the Holy Spirit whispered to my soul, *Why don't you believe the Father wouldn't do the same with you?* I almost dropped to my knees. I realized I could take this compassion and grace I was feeling at that moment toward this hurting man and multiply it times infinity, and it wouldn't even come close to the depth of the Father's feeling for me.

 *There is nothing you can do to increase God's love for you, and there is nothing you can do to diminish it.*

God the Father is ever longing for you, Ted, the Holy Spirit continued. I had heard it said many times, but that day I came to understand it at a new depth. There is nothing you can do to increase God's love for you, and there is nothing you can do to diminish it.

FINAL THOUGHTS

My friend, in this journey of becoming a pure-hearted disciple of Christ, God will never abandon you. A passionate-hearted disciple will realize this at some point and be gripped with a determined intimacy—the determined intimacy of God the Father.

If you walk in the way of trusting Him and His Word to you despite your feelings and emotional baggage from the past, then you will never abandon Him. You will be able to speak to the dry valley situations that come into your life. You will see lives changed, even lives at the point of despair. And the Word of God will truly sanctify you in the truth, as Jesus prayed in John 17.

Let's evaluate how you are dealing with and responding to God's truth. Read each statement and circle the number that best corresponds to your answer.

1. I feel I can totally trust God; He accepts even my weaknesses.

I struggle		I am not sure		All the time
1	2	3	4	5

2. I have a system of reading through the Bible each year.

No		Yes, but I rarely do it		Yes
1	2	3	4	5

3. I sense God the Father speaking to me and encouraging me as I read His Word.

Never		Rarely		Regularly
1	2	3	4	5

4. I struggle with believing God's promises to me.

Frequently		Every now and then		Never
1	2	3	4	5

5. God has used me to speak His healing and encouraging words to others!

I can't think of a time		I am not sure		Frequently
1	2	3	4	5

Score _____ (Add together the numbers you circled.)

This score will be added to the results from chapter 9 and the total score for Truth will be entered in the appropriate space on the Discipleship Development Analysis Tool in chapter 12.

CHAPTER NINE

THE BATTLE WITH THE MATRIX

Contending for God's Truth in Spiritual Battle

*Make [put your name here] holy, purify and heal and make
[put your name here] wholly yours by means of the truth. Your
Word is the consecrating and healing truth.*

(SEE JOHN 17:17.)

Jesus prayed passionately in John 17 that we would be sanctified, or set apart, in the truth. But truth does not go uncontested in our world, especially today. Discipleship is a determined intimacy with Christ and a determined battle with hell. It is a battle on three fronts—struggles with our flesh, the world system and the devil.

The moment you bring up the issue of spiritual warfare,

many people respond in extremes. Some simply deny the existence of spiritual warfare, despite all of the scriptural passages that clearly point to its reality in our world. In fact, the passages are so numerous and widespread it is not a question of whether we are engaged in spiritual warfare, the question is how effectively we are fighting (see 2 Kings 6:8-17; Acts 4:31-34; Eph. 6:10-18; Jas. 5:13-18; Rev. 12:7-11). Those who ignore the overwhelming biblical evidence respond by seeing everything within the confines of human logic and reason. They answer in naturalistic terms, totally excluding the realm of angelic and demonic forces.

Others fly off to the other extreme, seeing demons everywhere. They become official "Holy Ghost" demon chasers. But we are not battling just a bunch of demons; instead, we are battling a *world system!* Jesus made this clear in John 14:

> The prince of this world is coming. He has no hold on me, but the world must learn that I love the Father and that I do exactly what my Father has commanded me (vv. 30-31).

THE MATRIX AND OUR FALLEN EXISTENCE

Christ came to face the prince or ruler of our world system. The best depiction I have ever seen of this system, in parable form, was the movie *The Matrix.* Yes, it was an R-rated movie. I don't support or encourage attendance at R-rated movies, but the movie was the most disturbing and stunning depiction of spiritual truths I have seen in years. It was a graphic portrayal of where our world is today. It illustrated the forces we face, the mind games we deal with and the relentless pressures we feel.

When we don't realize we are battling a world system, we become extremely vulnerable. This lack of awareness sets us up to be blindsided. The world system aggravates the battle we have with our flesh, or self-centeredness, by providing and promoting opportunities for indulgence.

> *Discipleship is a determined intimacy with Christ and a determined battle with hell.*

In case you didn't see the movie, the story line will sound strangely familiar. Supercomputers have created a false computer image of the past called the Matrix, which is used to enslave human beings. Machines with artificial intelligence have taken over the world and are literally growing human beings as an energy crop. Neo, the main character, has a hard time buying into the fact that his world is an illusion. He thinks he is in control of his life. Morpheus explains to Neo he is not in control because of the Matrix. He tells him, "You feel it when you go to work or go to church or pay your taxes. It is the world that has been pulled over your eyes to blind you to the truth." "What truth?" Neo asks. "That you are a slave, Neo. That you, like everyone else, was born into bondage . . . kept inside a prison that you cannot smell, taste, or touch. A prison for your mind. Unfortunately, no one can be told what the Matrix is. You have to see it yourself," Morpheus responds.

Then Morpheus offers Neo the choice of two pills. Neo studies the pills in Morpheus's hands. In his right hand is a red pill; in his left hand is a blue pill. "You take the red pill and I show you how deep the rabbit hole goes. Remember that all I am offering you is the truth, nothing more," Morpheus solemnly says.

And the parable deepens. Neo takes the red pill and wakes up realizing what is actually going on in his world. He discovers he is actually encased in a device that the machines use to suck the life out of him while his mind is fed a false view of reality. He looks up from his bondage and sees countless other human beings in the same condition. At this point in the movie I am saying to myself, *What a picture of our world!*

Now that Neo sees the truth, he pulls himself up and begins to frantically unplug himself from all the connectors, hooks and chains that have been decimating his life. At this point I am fighting the urge to stand up and declare to everyone in the theater, "Folks, this is a picture of where all of us are spiritually without Christ. Turn to Him. He will not allow hell to suck the life out of you!" But my wife knew what I was thinking and leaned over and said, "Don't even think about it."

The most riveting aspect of the movie was the way in which it paralleled the biblical description of the world system we are fighting within the spirit. The Matrix was more than just the computer-generated reality being pumped into the heads of enslaved human beings to deceive them. It also expressed the rapacious character of the one who created the illusion—the one who was pulling the strings of slavery and deception. The Bible presents the devil as the mastermind of destruction in our world. He ruthlessly devours the souls of mankind but does it in such a way that those involved in the devastating process are blinded to what is actually going on in their life. Additionally, there are "gatekeepers," or "agents," in the movie—not your average adversaries—who enforce the deception. They seem to be indestructible and have incredible powers. Paul describes spiritual forces in Ephesians 6:12:

For our struggle is not against flesh and blood, but against the *rulers*, against the *authorities*, against the *powers* of this dark world and against the *spiritual forces* of evil in the heavenly realms (emphasis added).

There are powerful spiritual forces, or principalities, you have to wrestle with. But as in the movie, in Christ their power can be broken, yet it doesn't happen easily or overnight. Finally, just like the characters in the movie that have managed to break free, every time we attempt to help others come out of bondage we have to fight the agents in the false reality. Demons are the enforcers of the bondage of hell in our world.

The scene that stirred me the most was the final scene in the movie. Neo is in a phone booth. He finally has figured out how to deal with the gatekeepers. He picks up the phone and speaks to the Matrix, essentially saying, "Your days are numbered and your power is diminishing because the truth is being told!" And here is the best part—he steps outside the phone booth, adjusts his Hollywood shades and flies into the vertical. I'm thinking, *What a picture of a spirit-filled believer!*

THE CHALLENGES OF GOING VERTICAL

Now you might be saying to yourself, *Ted, thanks for the movie evaluation, but how does all of this apply to my life? How do I contend for God's truth in this crazy world?* Great question. Fortunately, Christ was very clear that our spiritual strength always will be found in servanthood, not in cerebral accomplishments:

If anyone would come after me, he must deny himself and take up his cross daily and follow me. For whoever wants to save his life will lose it, but whoever loses his life for me will save it (Luke 9:23-24).

If we have read the Bible at all, intellectually we know and understand servanthood is our calling in life. But it is not an easy sell to our hearts, because our own inadequacies can easily pull us away from that focus.

I was speaking at a large conference where I was doing a workshop. All the big-name speakers were doing general sessions. Dr. Ogilvie had just shared at one of the major sessions. Have you ever heard that guy speak? He almost sounds like God on a good day. His voice is incredible! It was my turn to share with participants in the workshop, and I was struggling. I sounded like Mickey Mouse—you know, that high, thin squeaky voice. Everyone had just spent a spellbound hour with Dr. Ogilvie, and I spent over an hour twisting in the wind. It was pitiful.

Why did I end up feeling like that? Because I was focused on myself again. I should have reached over and pulled out another one of those connectors the Matrix had reinserted into my skull. Hell tells us that if someone else is better than we are, then we are less. This is a battle I have revisited frequently in my life. Through the years I have found something that really helps me. I have this picture in my office at home. Actually, it is several pictures in one. It includes a pen-and-ink rendering of every aircraft I flew in the military—from the training aircraft to the deadly instruments of war. It also contains a few medals I received for staying alive. It reminds me of several pivotal times in my life. To make a long story short, the picture reminds me that *I am a dead man*. The only reason I came home alive was by the grace of God, not by my great flying ability or smarts. The truth is, it is the same for you. No matter what your background may be, your next breath is *courtesy of God*.

Every time I arrive back at that truth, it corrects my perspective in life. Once I am reminded of what God's grace has done in my life, then it doesn't matter if anyone recognizes me. I don't have to be special, because I already am. When I remember where I came from, I am just glad to be alive and be here. If you remember that truth about yourself when the enemy attacks—and he will—it can actually become a point of encouragement. I don't know about you, but sometimes I have no idea if I am being effective or not. I just keep showing up and trying to do what God has asked me to do. I just keep on walking. Then I realize I must be doing something right because the enemy is fighting me every step of the way. I am on his most wanted list. He is firing a lot of ammunition my way. You don't shoot at someone who isn't dangerous to you. You wouldn't waste the effort. Apparently I am getting to him. That is great! Hopefully, someday I will mature to the place that when I wake up in the morning, hell will say, "Oh, no, he is awake. We are in trouble!" That is when I'll know I'm really vertical.

CRAZY TIMES AND BOLD MEASURES

We live in crazy times—times of megachange and anxiety. From the airport check-in, which now reflects hypersecurity concerns instead of customer concerns, to the evening news, we live in crazy times! But that is nothing new. Joshua in the Old Testament was living in equally perilous times. Such times always present you with two options: (1) further chaos provoked by the instability of the situation or (2) massive breakthrough. Joshua always chose the latter. He knew how to speak the truth in the midst of crazy times.

Boldly Believing God's Truth

Now, as is so often the case today, the people he was dealing with frequently considered the truth to be optional. The Gibeonites, energized by the fear of their enemies the Amorites, denied who they really were and lied to Joshua. Several years ago I finally realized that the vast majority of folks that walk into the sanctuary on the weekend are dealing with addictions, bondage, deep family dysfunctions or "reparenting" issues. They are wrestling with huge enemies of the soul. Our flock at East Hill has a strong emphasis on reaching out to the unchurched and the dechurched, so it is to be expected that people with these struggles show up. But the truth is, traditional church folks today are not much different. They have just learned how to hide behind religious language.

Because of our extensive healing ministry in the area of sexual bondage, we have ministered to a great number of pastors who have fallen morally. And I have never counseled a leader or pastor caught with a fishhook from hell who initially told me the *whole* truth. Never! That is why we eventually started requiring fallen pastors to take a lie detector test up front if they wanted us to help them. Not because they were such evil men, but like the Gibeonites, their fear of being found out was making the truth optional.

In Joshua 10, Joshua finds himself bound to the Gibeonites because of his promise to them, despite the fact that they lied to him. His word and commitment were something that Joshua would not casually cast aside, despite the deception of others. This is a huge challenge in our world today, but it becomes much easier when you remember your calling as a servant—a disciple of the Lord. Joshua understood his calling clearly, even ministering to folks that weren't telling him the truth.

How desperately our land needs men and women like Joshua

today. He was a seasoned warrior. You always can tell when soldiers know what they are doing in battle. You can pick them out in the room as they start to suit up for a mission. You can tell just by the way they carry themselves. And you can definitely pick them out in a spiritual battle:

> On the day the LORD gave the Amorites over to Israel, Joshua said to the LORD in the presence of Israel: "O sun, stand still over Gideon, O moon, over the Valley of Aijalon." So the sun stood still, and the moon stopped, till the nation avenged itself on its enemies (Josh. 10:12-13).

In the heat of battle, before Joshua consulted with his men, before he double-checked the condition of his equipment and resources, he cried out to God. And he did so in front of everyone. He realized a critical truth we can easily forget when the spiritual bullets are flying. We are only as mighty as the anointing of God on our life. That is why we can be so awesome one moment and fall flat on our face the next. It is not because God is capricious with His empowering presence, but because under pressure we can forget who is in charge. God is in charge, not us. That truth must remain central in our thinking, despite the pressures we face; otherwise, servanthood will be perceived as an option.

Boldly Praying God's Truth

Just as important, Joshua was seasoned enough in the Lord to realize when the battle had come to a critical turning point. He realized when he was on the edge of a breakthrough—on the edge of an awesome victory. He was not just dealing with a league of kings coming against him. He was running out of time;

the sun was going down. The darkness would allow the enemy to escape and attack him again another day. We feel that same stress today—the feeling we are running out of time in our daily lives and activities and running out of time to defeat the enemies that keep us from profoundly experiencing God's truth and victory in our lives.

> *The feeling we are running out of time in our daily lives keeps us from profoundly experiencing God's truth and victory in our lives.*

Many times I have heard someone say to me, "But Pastor Ted, I just don't have time to study God's Word or pray or serve like I want to." The busyness of our culture frequently leaves us with little time to breathe, let alone experience significant spiritual victories. But Joshua would not settle for such a state of affairs. He cried out not just for a victory but also for God to coordinate such a crushing series of victories that his enemies would be shattered.

That is when he made a critical decision. He started praying the truth *boldly!* He didn't just believe in the truth, he contended for it. Contending for God's truth in a tough situation is not just about defending some old tradition. God's truth is ever alive and ever the same. Praying the truth boldly in the midst of a spiritual battle frequently will challenge you to ask God to do what He has never done before in your life. It is one thing to ask God to do what He has done before, but it is another thing entirely to ask God to create a new way. Crazy times call for bold people to boldly pray the truth.

Joshua prayed, "Lord, stop the sun and moon." No one before had ever prayed such a prayer. Bring fire from heaven, sure; bring the rain on drought-ravaged Israel, no problem. Send bread from heaven. What do you want, whole wheat or rye? But stop the sun and moon in the sky—now that is definitely different!

I remember the first time I read that prayer in Scripture. My undergraduate work was in mathematics and astrophysics. When I read that passage, I found myself thinking, *Wait just a minute. This is the sun we're talking about—a flaming ball of hydrogen and helium over 90 million miles from Earth and containing 99.9 percent of all the matter in our solar system. You can't control something like that! It is unreachable!* Then I realized that was the problem—my attitude. To be more precise, that was the core of the problem.

THE CORE OF THE PROBLEM

Joshua was crying out to God to do what only He could do. Joshua was doing everything he could with what he was facing, but he couldn't do anything about the sun going down. He was saying, "God, I am not asking You to help me a little. I am asking You to help me *a lot!* I am asking You to stop the sun, which is the center of the problem." In times of violent change and spiritual warfare, we need boldness to pray the truth:

> *Lord, this is beyond my abilities. I am doing everything I can, but without Your powerful help, it just isn't going to happen.*

However, we so frequently are distracted by the immediate problem—our kids are acting up; our job is in jeopardy; we seem to be drifting apart from our spouse. Because of our distractions, we simply pray about the immediate problem. We pray passionately, but we are not getting to the core of the problem. The kids are acting up because we have our job, our hobby or our hurts from the past in front of them. Only praying for the kids will never get to the core of the problem. The kids are a symptom of a bigger problem. Our job may seem to be in jeopardy, because God is putting it in jeopardy. He is asking us to trust Him, because He is changing the overall direction of our life. Yet we have a hard time seeing the good because we have come to believe we are what we do. And we can pray about our marriage falling apart, yet long before I have seen anyone drift away from their mate, they have drifted from God.

> *You can't put the enemy under your feet if you stay where you have always been.*

For example, in 25 years of marriage counseling, I have never had to counsel a couple that prays together each night. In fact, I used to ask couples that came in for counseling, "Do you two pray together each night?" "No! Why?" was their usual response. We have to love God's truth in order to pray about the core issues of life. A passionate-hearted disciple will pray bold prayers and will not be excited about the status quo. You see, you can't put the enemy under your feet if you stay where you have always been.

THE NECESSITY OF TAKING A RISK

Earlier in Joshua's story, we discover that he led his men in an all-night march. And it wasn't some stroll through the park. It covered many miles of rough terrain in the night. The army would have had to leave behind heavy weapons and then face a determined enemy at daybreak when they were fatigued. But the enemy never expected anyone would take that kind of risk. The anointing of God—the blessing of God—doesn't come if we don't take a risk. We will never be able to experience the truth of God in our lives apart from trusting in God's grace.

That was the character of God's response to Joshua, wasn't it? Joshua received time he was never supposed to have, time he had no right to ask for. He was asking for time expressed in grace. God always knows how to stop the hellish system that is working against you: by His grace. If you will boldly pray the truth of His grace over your situation, God will do His part.

However, that wasn't the end of the battle. In fact, the most important part of the conflict had yet to take place.

> Joshua said: "Open the mouth of the cave and bring those five kings out to me." So they brought the five kings out of the cave—the kings of Jerusalem, Hebron, Jarmuth, Lachish and Eglon. When they had brought these kings to Joshua, he summoned all the men of Israel and said to the army commanders who had come with him, "Come here and put your feet on the necks of these kings" (Josh. 10:22-24).

When Joshua brought out the captured kings, he vividly illustrated a critical principle in dealing with this world's demonic system. During the heat of the battle, the five kings had hidden in a cave. They saw where the battle was going and ran for cover to hide and lie low. It would have been so easy in the thrill of victory for Joshua to ignore or forget about the kings, who posed no immediate threat. However, you can win the battle and *still lose the war* for one simple reason: You didn't take care of the remnants in your life. Conversely, if you pray boldly, then you are someone who has dealt boldly with the remnants in your life. Truth is always relational, which is especially true in your life personally.

What are the remnants in your life? They are those little nagging leftovers from battles of the past, quiet struggles within that no one knows about. No one knows except you. And that is why you cannot declare God's truth boldly in your life. Of course, some folks go into hyperreligious denial and sound like they are speaking the truth, but their words fall flat in the face of hell's attacks.

Oh, the remnants probably are not much in the eyes of men. Those moments when you used to get really angry. Those moments when the old wolf of lust or rage growled in subdued tones from the cave of your soul. The old battles you used to have with food, depression or a need to control things. They are not much. I'm not talking about things people would ever know about you, because they really don't know. But God does; He knows all about you. Do you think God would have gone through all He did for you on the cross—literally blocking the sun in the sky—in order to allow the sins of the world—your sins and mine—to settle on the soul of His Son? Do you think that He would deal with all the demonic enemies of your soul and move supernaturally in your life? Do you think He would do all of that and *not deal* with remnants in your life—those remnants in your life that will one day grow into an army to once again destroy you? *I don't think so!* That is why it is critical you learn to speak the truth about yourself against the demonic systems of this world.

Now that is never an easy task in this world, especially if you come from a hurting home. Troy's life is a classic example of what I am referring to. (I have his permission to share his story.)

As a youngster he and his two brothers went to school every day with bruises and belt-buckle marks on their backs. Troy grew up seeing his father break his mother's nose and face countless times. He came to hate his father and fear his voice.

Troy came to Christ when he was around seven years of age. There was a Sunday School a block from his home, and he would take his brothers every Sunday. He prayed daily that his dad would stop beating his mom. For years he prayed that his dad would change and start loving his family. But nothing changed. The situation only grew worse, and slowly hell began to steal away his faith in God. He managed to escape his home when he was 18. When the holidays came, he returned home to visit the family. And once again, he saw the familiar signs of abuse against his mother and brothers. He told his brother to load his gun to protect the family. Soon he heard his father's truck coming down the driveway. The sons hid their mother. Their father was drunk, and as he entered the house, he started screaming that he was going to beat Troy if he didn't tell him where his mother was. I will never forget Troy as he stood before our flock with tears streaming down his face and uttered the following phrase: "That night was the last time I spoke to my dad, because my brother and I shot and killed him."

There was a stunned silence in the auditorium as Troy spoke those words. In one of the services, people openly wept out loud. It was a staggering moment of truth in Troy's life. If you had met the young man you never would have guessed what he had lived through. He was a professional actor and a very gracious man— poised and the picture of having it together. But in the years since his father's murder, he had not learned the power of speaking God's truth boldly in his life. He and his brother were acquitted on grounds of self-defense, and the little town in which his family lived supported them. The victory had been won, but the battle in Troy's life was only beginning. The remnants of his past and what he had done were buried, but they gained strength over the years. Troy threw himself into acting, trying to lose himself in the characters he played; but the remnants of his past only grew more powerful. Soon he found himself drinking heavily and using cocaine. His marriage started falling apart. He still was using cocaine when he came to East Hill. I will always remember Troy coming up to me at a men's retreat and pouring out the story of all he had done. He brought out the things of hell that had so dominated his life, the ruthless dictators of shame and rage that had so ruled and tormented his life for years. They had grown into a fearful army in his soul. After he poured out his story, I told him it was time to put an end to the tormenting rule of these adversaries. We needed to put our foot down and declare God's grace to be true in his life. I held him and we wept together. But as is so frequently the case, those remnants have slippery necks. They are tough to defeat.

Troy commented, "Pastor Ted and I prayed and he said I was forgiven, but I still could not believe it. It is one of the Ten Commandments—thou shall not kill. But finally during a midweek service, Pastor Ted and his wife prayed for my wife and me, and that is when I finally knew I was forgiven, as the Holy Spirit came deeply into my heart." Troy came to understand in his soul that he had a loving Dad who loved him unconditionally—Father God. Finally, the remnants of what once ruled his life were defeated. The Matrix had been unhooked from his mind, and I think his wife needed to be standing beside him for it to take place. He needed to finally see the reality of what God was giving him—a new family and a new life, a life characterized by grace. Troy got what he felt he never deserved. And the truth is, we all do! That is the truth we need to declare boldly to the remnants of the past that try to rule all of our lives.

Let's finish our evaluation of how we are dealing with the issue of truth. Read each question or statement and circle the number that best corresponds to your answer.

1. In stressful situations I can avoid becoming self-focused even when I may feel insecure.

It's a real struggle		I can usually respond that way	No problem	
1	2	3	4	5

2. How aware are you of the fact that your next breath is courtesy of God?

Not usually aware		Aware of the fact	Very aware	
1	2	3	4	5

3. Is it hard for you to serve folks in Christ's name when they might not be telling you the whole truth?

Very difficult		At times I struggle	I can love them anyway	
1	2	3	4	5

4. Can you boldly ask God to deal with the real core issue in your life, or do immediate problems distract you at times?

I am easily distracted		I am not sure	I can boldly ask	
1	2	3	4	5

5. Have you identified the remnants in the caves of your life, those things from your past that raise up an army against you?

Not really		Somewhat aware		I can list them
1	2	3	4	5

Score _____ (Add together the numbers you circled.)
Enter score from chapter 8 _____
Total score _____ (Add together the scores from chapters 8 and 9.)

Take this total score for Truth and enter it in the appropriate space on the Discipleship Development Analysis Tool in chapter 12.

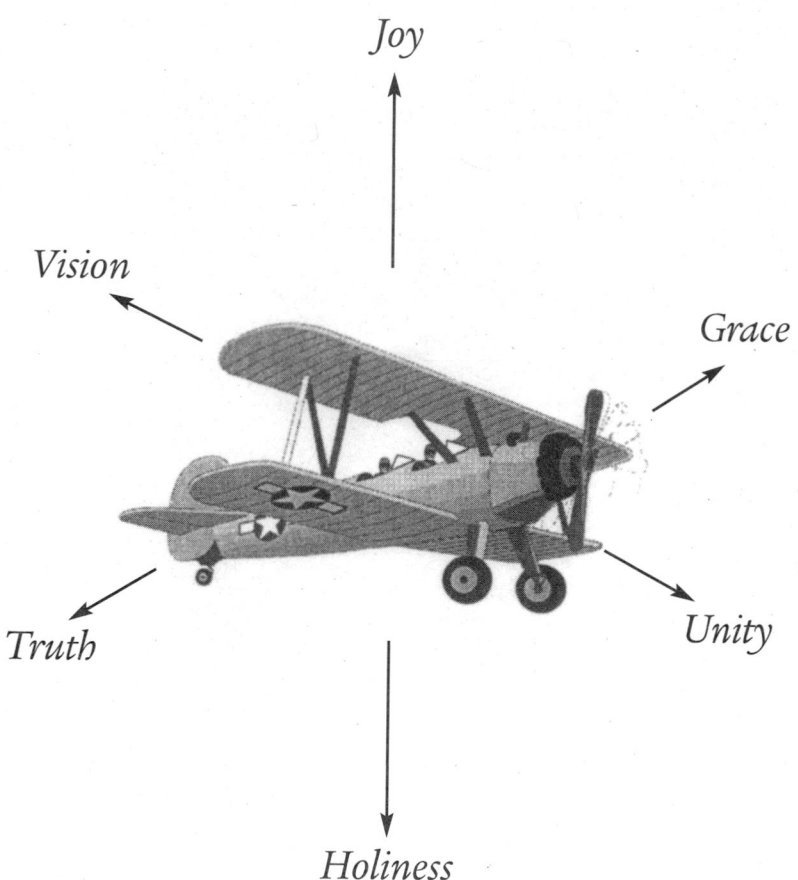

CHAPTER TEN

YOU ARE COMING THROUGH THIS

Following Our God-Given Vision in Life

*In the same manner that You sent Me into the world—with a clear
mission and purpose, I am sending* [put your name here] *with the
same mission and purpose. I have given Myself—consecrated
Myself totally to that purpose and mission so that*
[put your name here] *will be truth consecrated as well.*
(SEE JOHN 17:18-19.)

I was serving as a flight instructor in the naval training command and was given the task of training young men to fly high-performance fighter aircraft. The problem was that some of them couldn't even walk and chew gum at the same time, which could make for stressful flights. I had started intensely reading the Bible before I went to work, and that was especially true this day. I had a night formation flight that evening with three rookie pilots. My job was to keep them from running into one another or me over the darkened skies of south Texas.

My predilection for bottom-line data and information made the reading of Scripture tough sledding. I wasn't used to the terminology or culture context of the Bible, and I was just coming to know the heart of God. One of the things I love about the Lord is that He will make Scripture so simple even I can understand it. I was trying to read through Romans 8 when suddenly I understood that in Christ we all have been adopted. That might not mean much to you, but it was a staggering truth to me. I grew up thinking I was an illegitimate child. However, I learned that night that there are no illegitimate children, only illegitimate parents. Every child is a direct gift from God. Suddenly that feeling of illegitimacy, which had been a constant shaming factor to my soul, disappeared. Freedom came to my heart that day. And in the same instant, I heard the Lord whisper to my soul, *If you ever fly again, you will do it without Me. I am calling you into the pastoral ministry. I want you to minister to people who don't know they are My people.*

There is no way I could ever describe the shock of those words to my heart. I had never ever before considered being in the ministry. I was a career Marine Corps officer and fighter pilot. I had my career path clearly planned and being in ministry had never appeared on my radar screen. Yet God's stealthy grace flew right past my defenses and grabbed my heart, leading me down a different path than the one I had planned.

I did officially fly one time after I resigned from the military. I served as a copilot in a church's airplane for one flight. They couldn't find anyone to fly right seat, and I needed to get where they were going. To make a long story short, we lost one engine and couldn't get the landing gear down on approach. I told the young pilot, "Oh, just land it gear up. I had to do it once in combat. It's not that bad." That is when all the blood drained right out of his face. I finally found a way to get the gear down; and after we managed to land, the young pilot was muttering to himself that he had never experienced so many emergencies in one flight.

I also flew another time in a glider. My family presented me with a birthday card simply entitled "Ted's Excellent Adventure." They had purchased a mile-high glider flight for me. As we approached the airfield, the instructor was standing in the field waiting for us. He was cussing a blue streak because we were a little late for the scheduled flight. My kids were stunned, but to me it felt like old times being around planes and profanity. The instructor continued cussing profusely all the way up to altitude during the tow. Just prior to release, he asked me if I had any flight experience. I shared with him my flight background, to which he replied, "Okay, you can take the aircraft once we disconnect from the tow plane. Let's see what you can do." I had never flown a glider before, so I had a ball.

After a few minutes of silently soaring, he asked me what I did for a living. "Well, I'm a pastor. I have been in that line of work for about 10 years," I cautiously replied. There was a long, uncomfortable silence. Then he asked, "What do you pass?" I kid you not, that is exactly what he said to me. "I guess you could say I am a preacher," I continued. That set him off, and once again the cockpit was awash with profanities. Then he finally calmed down enough to ask, "How in the —— did you end up becoming a preacher with all your flying background?" For the next 30 minutes, I shared all the miracles, struggles and supernatural victories in my life; I held nothing back. As I shared, I was reminded of the words God whispered to my soul that day over a decade before: *I want you to minister to people who don't know they are My people.* The God-given vision was coming to pass.

A GOD-GIVEN VISION WILL GIVE PURPOSE

Few things bring stability and courage to the human soul like having a sense of divine mission and purpose. Truth, even divine truth, can't simply remain an intellectual pursuit. The vicissitudes of life will vitiate our finest mental constructs. Without a sense of vision, our most reasonable efforts will soon seem worthless. That is why it is so critical for us to understand this aspect of Christ's prayer, "I am sending them with a clear mission and purpose." Having a God-given vision is profoundly difficult at times, because vision is never just about us. Any God-given vision is about what God does in the lives of others through our sacrifice and service to Him. A God-given vision always has to do with the way we relate to others, especially the difficult others. All of the profanity flying my way that day wasn't easy to deal with, but it was more than worth it once the pilot asked me to share my experiences in Christ. Conversely, living life without a God-given vision eventually becomes an exercise in futility and frustration.

It doesn't matter how many toys or awards you may pick up along the way, they are meaningless unless you are headed somewhere of eternal significance. Helen Keller was asked what would be worse than being born blind. She quickly replied, "To have sight and no vision."[1]

I love the way George Barna writes books that analyze statistical facts concerning the Church. He has become an accounting prophet to the Church in America. However, he is not just a bean counter, because in the haystack of statistical stuff, he always manages to find a prophetic needle of insight. For example, he recently reported that three-fourths of the pastors in America don't feel they are called or have ever had a specific vision from the Lord.[2] That nearly brought tears to my eyes because the poorest person in the world is not the person without a nickel to his name. The poorest person is the one who does not have a God-given vision or dream. When you are without vision and trying to lead a ministry, it is nothing but grinding futility.

Few things bring stability and courage to the human soul like having a sense of divine mission and purpose.

A GOD-GIVEN VISION WILL BE DISTINCT

In Acts 26, Paul stands before King Agrippa and makes his defense with respect to the false charges being leveled at him by the Jews. In the process, he shares Christ's call in his life and adds this clarion comment:

> So then, King Agrippa, I was not disobedient to the vision from heaven (v. 19).

At the core of Paul's ability to handle the abuse, disappointments and unmet expectations he so frequently faced in life was his God-given vision. He never lost sight of the prize and purpose of his life.

In Acts 9, Saul, soon-to-be Paul, ends up face planting as God redirects his life. He has an encounter with the risen Christ, and if we look carefully, we will see a pattern that is true for every

God-given vision. Visions that come from the heart of God will always bear His distinct signature. A godly vision will be distinct from a lot of visions you hear people talk about today. In most cases, those visions are nothing more than learned optimism, which usually is based on business or human-potential models with religious language thrown in to make them sound spiritual. But God has a much better plan:

> As he neared Damascus on his journey, suddenly a light from heaven flashed around him. He fell to the ground and heard a voice say to him, "Saul, Saul, why do you persecute me?" "Who are you, Lord?" Saul asked. "I am Jesus, whom you are persecuting," he replied. "Now get up and go into the city, and you will be told what you must do" (Acts 9:3-6).

A GOD-GIVEN VISION WILL GRAB YOU

A God-given vision initially will stop you in your tracks. The first thing that will happen is you clearly will see where you are. Now, I didn't say *who* you are but *where* you are. As I prayed years ago, I came to realize I was totally out of God's will by being a flight instructor. It wasn't a comfortable revelation. All I had ever wanted to do in life was fly, but I had never bothered to check with God to see if He had designed something else for my life. I never sought to ask the question, Is Your vision for my life the same as my vision? It is painful to realize you are out of line with God's vision for your life. And the *where* must never be confused with the *who*. You first have to see the where clearly to understand the who. It will feel like bad news initially, but bad news becomes irrelevant as you realize that God always has the best plan in store for you.

There are some moments that will stay with me forever—blasting off the end of the runway early in the morning with thrust to burn; pulling the aircraft straight up into the vertical and climbing out of sight, landing aboard an aircraft carrier and everything goes just right; being tucked up underneath three other aircraft "in the slot" and aileron-rolling in diamond formation over the airfield; corkscrewing through the sky with another aircraft only a few feet away and the sun glistening off of it. However, all of those moments are absolutely insignificant compared to being in the midst of one of our five weekend services and sensing the Lord giving me a divine "Hooray! Way to go, Ted; this is what I made you for!" Nothing compares to living your life from the perspective of a God-given vision. Absolutely nothing!

Initially, a God-given vision is a discouraging look, because we realize where we have truly ended up in life by our own efforts. Even our good efforts can have us arriving at the wrong place. The prophet Isaiah is a classic illustration of this truth. In Isaiah 1—5, he preached to the people of Israel, and then he suddenly saw *where* he was. His response was, "Woe to me!" (Isa. 6:5). Isaiah almost got stuck there—until God helped him to see *who* he really was. He was a man sent by the hand of God with a God-given vision.

The first step in any God-given vision is repentance. Now that is not a negative word, despite the fact that a lot of church folks have tried to turn it into a condemning word. Don't make the mistake of getting caught up in the "I am a worm" theology: "Oh, I am nothing. Woe is me." Even the evolutionists believe we are more than a worm!

God will not allow you to see yourself and your problems without also showing you your potential. Conversely, God can easily deal with us if we get too prideful. He who gets too big for his britches will be exposed in the end! The deepest levels of repentance are usually about us having too low an opinion of what God can do through us. If we have honestly said yes to Christ, then we are loved of God, treasured of God and filled with the Holy Spirit—designed by heaven to be hell's worst nightmare and handcrafted by God to make a difference in our world! Most of us need to repent for having lived far below our spiritual potential and gifting. We need to let God's dream and vision for us really grab us!

A GOD-GIVEN VISION WILL CHALLENGE YOU

Once you realize just how big God's dream for your life actually is, you will be challenged to the very core of your being. Visions built on human potential and self-effort ultimately are about self-gratification. They will never go deep enough to touch the very character of your soul. Such visions tend to deal with external accomplishments or achievements rather than the things we carry out of this life—character and relationships. Everything else will fade away no matter how significant it may appear in today's world, but character builds hope. That is why hope is the fuel God-given dreams run on.

It is hope that provokes a bride and groom to stand at the altar and promise, "I do," even when there are no guarantees. It is hope that provokes parents to bring children into a fallen world that seems to be getting further from God with each passing day. It is hope that inspires us to face a habit that has mocked us for years as we have tried to follow God. It is hope that allows us to look at our nation and sense there has never been a better time for a true revival to sweep the land.

A God-given dream is a fascinating symphony of struggles

and victories all orchestrated by the hand of God. You see this clearly in God's instructions to Ananias as he is sent to pray over a bewildered Paul:

> Go! This man is my chosen instrument to carry my name before the Gentiles and their kings and before the people of Israel. *I will show him how much he must suffer for my name* (Acts 9:15-16, emphasis added).

> *A God-given dream is a fascinating symphony of struggles and victories all orchestrated by the hand of God.*

There is something absolutely awesome about the dreams of God. The dreams of God only grow stronger in the dark times of life. Many times I have felt like walking away from the ministry. But about the time I get out the front door something in my heart pulls me right back into the battle. I have quit so many times on Monday morning that my secretary has developed a resignation form letter I can sign each week. Of course, she never submits it because she knows that come Tuesday morning I will be ready to get back into the fray!

Any problem is an overwhelming problem when there is no hope. But no problem, no matter how big it is, is a problem when there is hope. And it is in the tension of these two extremes that God-given visions are born.

A GOD-GIVEN VISION IS ULTIMATELY BIRTHED IN THE DARK TIMES OF LIFE

Christ allows circumstances to welcome us into the dark times of life. Most of the time we come into the shadows of life kicking and screaming, but we need to remember we are in great company. God did some of His greatest work in David's life when David was hiding in a cave from a crazed King Saul. God spoke some of His most profound truths through the pen of the apostle Paul as he hunched over a flickering candle in his final Roman prison cell. The cell was nothing more than a hole in the ground. And I think for most of us, God speaks His deepest truths to us when we find ourselves in a jail cell—a cave of our own making. In my opinion, there is no greater illustration of that fact than the encounter Jesus had with the woman in John 8.

The Pharisees are playing their power games as usual. They have managed to entrap a woman in the very act of adultery. Essentially, they have treated her like a thing or sex object in order to get at Christ:

> The teachers of the law and the Pharisees brought in a woman caught in adultery. They made her stand before the group and said to Jesus, "Teacher, this woman was caught in the act of adultery. In the Law Moses commanded us to stone such women. Now what do you say?" But Jesus bent down and started to write on the ground with his finger (John 8:3-6).

Sometimes Jesus is just too awesome for words! I love how He deals with these self-righteous men. They have torn what little shreds of dignity this woman has apart, humbling her down to the depths of her soul. I mean, can you imagine just how shaming that must have been for her to stand there? When the Pharisees continued their abuse, Jesus just blows them apart:

> "If any one of you is without sin, let him be the first to throw a stone at her." Again he stooped down and wrote on the ground (John 8:7-8).

Now here is the part I especially enjoy: The text tells us every one of those troglodytic men dropped the rocks in their hands and ran for the hills. I get a kick out of the fact that the text also tells us the older men started leaving first. That must have been an incredibly powerful message Jesus wrote in the sand. I have been asked many times, "Pastor Ted, what did Jesus write in the sand?" That is a great question, because John tells us Jesus wrote something, but he doesn't tell us what it was. Whatever it was, it blew those self-righteous men away.

Let me tell you what Jesus wrote in the sand. I really know what it was. *But how can you say that?* you're probably thinking. Simple. The woman was brought to Jesus for breaking the Law with respect to adultery. Now adultery is kind of tough to pull off as a solo act. The man should have been standing there as well, because Scripture tells us she was caught in the very act of adultery (see John 8:4). What is clearly taking place is entrapment. Additionally, for anyone to be qualified to throw a stone, it was understood they could not have been involved in such an act themselves. Jesus was not asking for those who were perfect to step forward. Instead, He was asking those who had never struggled with the same issue in their own life to please step forward.

I picture the scene this way. The oldest guy steps forward—the elder in the community. He has this huge rock in his hand ready to strike the cowering, frightened woman. Right at that moment, Jesus leans forward and writes "Ruth" in the sand. In a flash the rock is dropped and the man heads for the hills. The next man boldly steps forward lifting his rock-loaded right hand to bludgeon the helpless woman. Jesus leans forward and writes "Josephine" in the sand. Another rock falls harmlessly to the ground. Now we are down to the young bucks. A young hothead leaps forward to strike the woman and Jesus leans forward almost with a smile on his face and writes "Betty Lou" in the sand. You get the picture. Jesus looks right into the soul of each man, confronting their fears and hypocrisy and then pointing the way to wholeness. He walked into their personal caves and pointed the way out without condemnation.

Can you imagine how that hurting woman must have felt? Probably for the first time in her life she hadn't been treated as a thing or a sex object. In the midst of the darkest time of her life, Christ was there to comfort her, not to condemn her. He didn't condone her past life; instead, He called to her in her cave of shame, bidding her to come to God's vision for her life.

A GOD-GIVEN VISION WILL SPUR YOUR SOUL TO ACTION

As you have seen, a God-given vision will initially grip our soul with the revelation of where we really are in life. Then God will begin to show us where He will take us in life, which will scare "the tar" out of us. Yet the tension of the grip of God on our life and the fear of our own inabilities and frustrations will at some point lead us into a cave of personal disappointments. It is there we discover God is uniquely with us—our defender from those who would stone us. He also is our encourager when we aren't so much ducking stones but feeling like throwing in the towel ourselves.

No matter where we may be in this spectrum, at some point we will have to take action. God's grace never comes to us so that we can just sit on the sidelines in life. Instead, He calls us to significance. In areas where we struggle with fear—it could be the fear of accusing rocks from others or it could be the fear of personal failure over the frustration of not seeing the vision come to pass—the single most destructive thing we can do is nothing.

In a delightful little book *Art and Fear*, a ceramics teacher divides her class into two groups. One group is graded solely on the *quantity* of work produced—the more pots produced, the higher the grade. The other group is graded solely on *quality*—doesn't matter if they produce only one pot, but it has to be very good. What is amazing about this little experiment is the fact that the first group, the quantity group, produces all the superb pots.[3] The reason is rather obvious once you stop and think about it. The sharp students in the quantity group kept learning from their mistakes. They grew as artists. On the other hand, the quality group was so consumed with their need for perfection that they didn't get any better. What a picture of life!

Keep On Keeping On

God can turn the many mistakes we make in life into learning experiences. Each of our lives is littered with mistakes, mess-ups and just plain old sin. Life is a road cluttered with our imperfections; but there is no other road, otherwise we wouldn't continually be in need of a Savior. While the clutter from our sense of failure in life can drive us into a cave of fear and frustration, God is still there for us. That is what gives us hope. That is why we can persist in life—why we keep on keeping on when the energy of self-promotion has long since faded or soured.

Probably one of the most moving illustrations of this truth is found in the life of David. In Samuel 24, David has been hiding for years from Saul. Saul unknowingly comes to the very cave where David is, but he can't see him. In fact, he ends up only a few feet away from David. David's men are telling him that this is a sign from God. He should rise up, kill Saul and take over as king. The dialogue probably sounded something like this: "This man has tormented you for years. God has told you that you are the next king. Just kill the guy!" However, David wouldn't do it. In the negativity of that cave, a staggering positive was revealed in David's life. *David wanted to belong to God more than he wanted to be king.* The God-given vision in David's life was being clarified and developed. In the negativity of the caves of our life, God encourages us to hand the dream back to Him, so it can be cleaned off and developed. We all tend to get the fingerprints of our own personal ambition all over our God-given dreams. But God can use the dark times of our cave situations to develop the positive picture of His purpose in our life.

Rely on God as the Master Developer

Recently my family gave me a great present—a high-quality underwater camera. I soon discovered a number of things about taking pictures underwater. It is not easy to get the shots you see in all the diving magazines. Now the mechanics of a nondigital camera are pretty straightforward. The outside image is captured on the film in the back of the camera, *which creates a negative of the outside image.* But it takes a master to get the process just right and develop the pictures perfectly.

God is the master picture taker, and He starts with a negative. The initial picture is called a negative because whatever is light becomes dark, and whatever is dark becomes light. God—because of His decision to love mankind—built within us the capacity to reverse everything. We can choose the opposite of God's will, or we can choose to stay in alignment with God's will.

Love by its nature has built into it the freedom to choose, both good and bad. That is why when Adam *fell* God did not *fail*. God knew that Adam's negative choices didn't end the process.

What is my point? You may have struggled to understand the huge gap that exists in your life. When you look at God's promises in His love letters and then you look at yourself, you can't reconcile the promises and your performance! Any honest person finds themselves saying, "God, how can I be opposite of what you say I ought to be?" In the dark times of life, God will whisper to your soul, *I'm not through with you yet. The picture will come out of the negative.*

David's Darkroom Experience. King David was a passionate warrior and lover of God. But his passions also led him to make incredibly destructive choices in his life. Time and again the negative things you see people struggling with in Scripture become incredibly positive once they turned around. For example, Paul's intellectual brilliance initially blocked him from realizing who Christ was. But once he ended up face first in the dirt on the road to Damascus—getting turned in the right direction—his mind soared on the wings of the Spirit as he took pen in hand and wrote the major part of the New Testament. Isn't it fascinating that God has a preference for murderers like Moses and David and for jailbirds like Paul and John? In fact, most of the New Testament was written by ex-cons. God doesn't just pick good people. It seems like He actually prefers "negatives."

Look at it this way. No one goes out and buys an expensive picture frame for a negative. You don't put negatives in your wallet or on the refrigerator. You would never do that because the image has not yet been developed. I am sure that if God has a wallet, your picture is in it; and if He has a refrigerator, your picture is in a place of honor on the front door. However, first God had to develop the negative of your life. The God-given vision He put in your soul is the finished picture. Part of living out your God-given vision is realizing that the negatives in your life have to be developed. The negatives are all the aspects of your life that will eventually be in the final picture, or vision, but they have yet to be developed. I think one of the best definitions of success is when believers fully develop their God-given vision before death catches them.

> *If God has a wallet, your picture is in it; and if He has a refrigerator, your picture is in a place of honor on the front door.*

Jacob's Darkroom Experience. Jacob, in the Old Testament, was the riverboat gambler of the patriarchs. He constantly dealt from the bottom of the deck and tried to figure the angles. He was the ultimate con man, an archetypal negative. But he ended up wrestling with God in the middle of the night, and in the process, God began to deeply develop the picture of His purpose within Jacob. He took Jacob to an emotional cave and brought forth not a crook but a prince. The darkrooms of life develop what God has placed in us as nothing else does.

Job's Darkroom Experience. Job had the ultimate darkroom experience. For nearly 35 chapters, Job ranted and raved at God over his pain. His friends, if you can call them friends, were strong developers God poured into the mixture of Job's anguish. They were like caustic solutions that the negatives of Job's life were dipped in. But when the picture came forth, it was one of the most stunning pictures of faith in the Old Testament, as Job cried out:

My ears had heard of you but now my eyes have seen you. Therefore I despise myself and repent in dust and ashes (Job 42:5-6).

It was in the darkroom of his deep disappointments that his mind transformed from an intellectual faith to an inner faith.

Find Your Vision in the Darkroom

If you will take a moment and look back over your life, you will make an amazing discovery. You will find some of the most significant times of spiritual growth in your life came in the caves—in the darkroom times of life. The reason for that is in the darkroom times of your life, God will develop character traits in you that you didn't even know you had. And no developer would just leave the film in the darkroom. If you are going through a tough time and have said yes to Christ, there is one thing you can absolutely count on—you are coming through this! God is going to take every single negative in your life and bring forth a powerful picture of His grace. That is why there will never be a time in your life when you will find yourself without hope.

The darkest time the world has ever seen occurred on what is strangely called Good Friday. Christ was publicly humiliated, shamed, spat upon and openly ridiculed. On a bloody, brutal Roman torture device, all of His dreams appeared to die. What began as an exuberant God-given vision ended in grinding agony. Then Jesus' body was placed in a tomb, a dark place, which was a huge mistake, because hell always thinks the darkness extinguishes God-given dreams. You know the rest of the marvelous story. On Sunday morning hell was blown apart. Hell's darkness became God's developing room. And it always will be if we will trust Him by persisting in our God-given vision.

Trust God to Carry You Through the Dark Times

The young lady stood before the flock and began to speak—initially with a faltering voice and then with an ever-increasing confidence. She had been sexually abused as a child. She had gone through numerous relationships and marriages, eventually marrying a pimp who prostituted her in a world of lust and greed. Finally, she ended up in a hospice, having been diagnosed with a terminal disease and only a few weeks to live. She continued by saying:

> I had been in the hospice a few days when one night, as I closed my eyes, I saw my life before me. As each event passed, I wept with deep sorrow. As I cried, I sensed a presence. A man stood with his arms outstretched toward heaven, tears flowing down his face. He was pleading—pleading for me. I knew it was Jesus. As I watched and waited, I realized He was praying for me! Then I saw the most wonderful glow. It was as if the heavens were glowing with the glory of God. Glory is not a word I have ever used, but it is the only word I can think of to explain this experience. I didn't die. Eventually, I was released from the hospice. At times the restoration has been hard work, even overwhelming. But Christ always meets me, giving me the strength and courage to go forward. It's through others sharing their darkroom times with me and loving me—when I could not love myself—that I've learned to live, love and trust again. You see, what I once believed were ordinary people placed in my life at the right times were really His extraordinary hands extended to me.

There weren't too many dry eyes in the house as I stood to

speak following her testimony. The deep emotional response to her words was not simply provoked by the depth of her pain but by the beauty of her God-given vision, a vision of Christ birthed out of the darkest times of her life, a vision calling her to first clearly realize where she was and how she got there. From that point forward, Christ spoke a hope in her heart that enabled her to persistently pursue Him. She took action and literally walked out of that hospice. Why? She finally realized who she was. Like the woman in John 8, she came to understand that despite her failures, she was outrageously loved of God. The greatest God-given vision of all is to live as someone deeply loved by God.

Let's evaluate how you are doing in agreeing with Christ's prayer for you that there is a God-given vision directing your life. Read each question and circle the number that best corresponds to your answer.

1. Has God helped you see where you really are in life?

Frequently		Occasionally		Infrequently
1	2	3	4	5

2. Do you feel that what you are doing for a living is at the center of God's will for you?

It's just a job		Not really		Absolutely
1	2	3	4	5

3. Do you sense that you have too low an opinion of what God could do through your life?

I'm not sure God has a positive opinion of me		Not sure		Not really
1	2	3	4	5

4. Are you someone who has been handcrafted by God to make a difference in this world?

I don't think so		Maybe		Yes, I am!
1	2	3	4	5

5. Is your God-given dream growing stronger with each passing year despite the dark times?

No		It's up and down		Yes, it is
1	2	3	4	5

6. How easy is it for you to trust God in the darkroom times of life?

Impossible		I white-knuckle it		I hang in there
1	2	3	4	5

7. Do you tend to beat yourself up when you make a mistake?

All the time		Occasionally		Almost never
1	2	3	4	5

8. How hopeful are you right now about your future?

Not very		Neutral		Really hopeful
1	2	3	4	5

9. Are you living like someone who is deeply loved by God?

Not really		At times		I think so
1	2	3	4	5

10. Do you feel God has taken a number of your negatives and turned them into a picture of His grace?

No, they still haunt me		Maybe		He is doing great job
1	2	3	4	5

Score _____ (Add together the numbers you circled.)

Take this total score for Vision and enter it in the appropriate space on the Discipleship Development Analysis Tool in chapter 12.

CHAPTER ELEVEN

COME TO THE PARTY

Creating Unity Within the Church

I am not just praying for those surrounding Me tonight, but also for those who will come to believe and trust in Me through their witness, so they would all be of one heart and one mind just as You, Father, are in Me and I in You. Then the world will believe that You did, indeed, send Me. I have given them the glory You gave to Me, for the purpose that they would be one as We are one. I in them and You in Me. Then they will mature in this unity and oneness to the place that a lost world will recognize that You sent Me.

(SEE JOHN 17:20-23.)

There are some moments as a dad that stay with you forever. Memories of laughter and discovery—memories of holding your son or daughter close and feeling one with them is priceless. The temporary insanity of the teen years can truly test your mettle as a dad, but the joy of watching them mature into young adults is worth it.

The *kairos*, or critical moments, for me were those times where I actually got it right as a dad, when I realized God was speaking to my soul through my kids. Now there are not a lot of moments like that in my memory, but one stands out with particular clarity. My son and daughter were fighting in the living room. One was in grade school and the other was close behind. I finally realized that a major conflict had broken out when a piercing scream interrupted my peaceful reading. They were at war over a toy and it was take no prisoners! Suddenly a flash of divine inspiration hit me. I called both belligerent parties over to my chair for consultation. Instead of trying to figure out who hit whom first, I simply said to them, "We don't do that in the Roberts's household. We don't treat each other like that. There is one rule around here—be a Roberts. That means you need to apologize to each other." They looked at me in disbelief and said, "Is that true, Dad?" "It sure is," I replied. "That is the way it works around here." They glanced at each other, then stiffly gave each other a hug and went back to playing. Soon they were acting as if nothing had ever happened. It was marvelous! And I think it lasted until bedtime.

The Holy Spirit spoke to me in those moments, not only of my love for my children, but also of God's love for me. I suddenly understood the relationship between Jesus' prayers for our unity in John 17 and our daily struggles with one another:

> Then they will mature in this unity and oneness to the place that a lost world will recognize that You sent Me

and You love them as much as You love Me (see vv. 22-23).

Paul's comments concerning unity in Ephesians 4 clearly show us the importance of our unity as believers. It is the key to a lost world—recognizing Jesus for who He actually is—our Savior, healer, Lord and coming King! But even more startling is the promise that when we as believers walk in the unity God purposes for us, people will come to understand how

Unity is the ultimate purpose—not for us to just grow up, but also for our world to be touched and changed because of our commitment to one another.

incredibly loved by God they are. Otherwise, they never will fully comprehend the outrageous love of God—that we are loved by God as much as He loves His Son. But that is precisely what Christ is asking to be released in our world through our unity. This is not an insignificant or secondary aspect of discipleship. The effort we put forth with respect to discipleship doesn't just affect our lives; it has a staggering effect on our world. That is why the Church must get this right. It is the ultimate purpose of this entire book—not for us to just grow up, but also for our world to be touched and changed because of our commitment to one another. Discipleship is never a solo experience or simply a personal-growth issue.

PAUL'S AMAZING REVELATION OF GOD'S LOVE

I vividly remember the first time I actually read what Paul had to say about unity among believers. I had read the passage hundreds of times before, but once I really read it, I was stunned. His wise, Spirit-inspired words resounded in my soul:

> As a prisoner for the Lord, then, I urge you to live a life worthy of the calling you have received. Be completely humble and gentle; be patient, bearing with one another in love. Make every effort to keep the unity of the Spirit through the bond of peace (Eph. 4:1-3).

What a marvelous symphony of words. "Worthy" means "living on a par with or equal to." But you have to ask the question, On a par with what? On a par with your calling—that is Paul's challenge. "Calling" is a word that unfortunately has been stolen from the everyday believer by the spiritual space cadets. However, the word isn't reserved for the few, the proud and the superspiritual. The Greek term, *kaleo*, simply refers to an invitation or a welcome to go.[1] Paul is telling us that every believer has received a calling from the Father. Every one of us who has said yes to Christ has had an e-mail from heaven flash on the computer screen of our heart saying something like this: "Dear Ted, you have been invited to a relationship with your heavenly Father that is characterized by *forgiveness*."

It doesn't matter how many times you have messed up or even how many times you have promised you wouldn't mess up and did anyway—you are forgiven. It also is a relationship characterized by *grace*. You get what you don't remotely deserve. It is a relationship characterized by *acceptance* and *mercy*. You don't get what you deserve, and you are accepted as well.

But above all, it is a relationship totally characterized by *love*. Your heavenly Father will not leave you the way you are. Your part is to be humble and gentle, bearing with one another in love. I can handle humble, but "gentle" is not an easy word to buy into as a guy. It sounds a bit too weak for me. But once again, the meaning of the original word is a far cry from the term's popular usage today. *Praus* is a magnificent word—the same word used by Christ in the Sermon on the Mount when He described the power of the meek. I love the definition of the word when it is used to refer to a horse that has been trained for battle.[2]

Several things are important to understand with respect to the word's usage in the first century. First of all, horses were not a common mode of transportation. A horse was reserved for the commander of the army to ride upon. For the commander to be able to function in the heat of battle, the horse was trained not to react to the sounds and chaos of the battle taking place around him. "Praus" is a powerful term to describe self-control under trying circumstances.

Additionally, "praus" is used to illustrate being patient and bearing with one another in love. It seems that Paul knew we would have trouble with one another at times. He sure ran into that problem in the churches he pastored! The bottom line in his admonition to us is, Before you lose your cool with a follower of Christ, just remember how patient God is with you. We are invited to relate to one another on the same level and in the same way that Christ treats us.

You may be thinking, *Oh, Ted, I know that. I have heard that a hundred times.* I know you have, but we still have a problem. A dear friend of mine started pastoring a small church in a metropolitan area that soon grew to be a significant church in the city. I get a kick out of how he got things turned around. When he first arrived, he preached essentially the same sermon for two months—love one another. Finally, a man came up to him and said, "Pastor, you have been giving us the same sermon for two months. When are you going to give us something new?" My friend smiled and said, "Once you start practicing it!" The flock got the message and things started to turn around.

God's Personal Invitation

So how do we respond to the enormity of Paul's word? Ephesians 4:3 tells us exactly how:

Make every effort to keep the unity of the Spirit through the bond of peace.

"Make every effort" tells us this is not a new thought but a continuation of what has been said before. Paul is helping us understand the reason we must treat each other as God has treated us, because it is the key to unity in the Church. Therefore—now don't miss this—unity in the Church is *already built right in*. It is built in because of Christ's actions and attitude toward us. Our problem is our orneriness keeps getting in the way, just as it did when my kids fought over a toy.

And it is our unity, not our programs, great worship services, buildings, evangelistic efforts or ministry to the poor that will reach the world. Instead, it is our unity that will reach a hurting and busted world and convince them of Christ's love. Therefore, the bottom line in discipleship—what ties everything we have learned together—is unity and vision. As believers, we need to realize that unity in the Church depends on our willingness to celebrate and work together to fully understand the marvelous invitation God has extended to us.

It is a personal invitation specifically given to each one of us—not some heavenly form letter written to appear personal. It is an engraved, bloodstained invitation from the nail-scarred hands of Christ. In other words, we must never lose sight of our personal invitation. We need to be constantly awed by the fact *Christ truly likes us!* Ever since I decided to follow Christ in the middle of a war years ago, I have believed that God loved me. But the fact that He personally liked me—well, that is a different story. It was a stretch for me to believe in His personal love for me, because frequently I didn't like what I did and I really didn't like myself. What I also seemed to forget was that God's personal invitation was characterized not just by His grace but His love as well, which meant He was not going to leave me the way I was. Our heavenly Father not only extends a personal invitation, He desires a personal relationship with each of us as well.

> *Our heavenly Father not only extends a personal invitation, He desires a personal relationship with each of us as well.*

I was on a bike tour through the steep terrain of Northern California. I was using the ride as a conditioning exercise for some upcoming triathlons. After a great ride, I arrived at the campsite before anyone else. I pulled my gear out of the trailer and began to set up my tent. But before I got involved in all the details of the setup, I collapsed and tried to recover from the fatiguing ride. As I sat there, I realized it had been a long time since I had just sat down and watched the clouds roll by. In fact, I hadn't done that since I was a kid in grade school. It suddenly hit me how driven my life had been. As I watched the cumulus clouds rumbling rapidly heavenward, pushed by the approaching front, I was awed by their power and beauty. That was when I sensed something far more powerful—the manifest presence of Christ. His presence was so intense that I knew if I turned my head I would see Him standing beside me. But I was never able to do that because I heard Him speak to my heart and say, *Ted, I really like you. In your busyness I have missed being with you.*

It is difficult to describe how those words impacted my soul. I fell apart. I began crying, nose running, you name it! I fell on my face as the words, "Ted, I really like you," echoed in my soul. I knew God loved me. He is supposed to; that is what God does. But he liked me? That was incredible! The fact that Christ's invitation to each of us is personal and not some legal notice stating we are forgiven is absolutely revolutionary once it hits our heart. It is critical for us to never lose that sense of personal invitation; otherwise, we will begin to treat each other in destructive, defensive and blaming ways. We will argue with each other over toys, even in God's house—the toys of pride, position and power, which make our witness to a hurting world ridiculous and irrelevant. Unfortunately, this type of behavior occurs in many of America's churches today, which is why our generation has pretty much turned a deaf ear to the Church.

Relationships

Once we lose sight of God's extended invitation to us, it affects our relationships. If we never sense the awe of Christ's profound affection for us, we will constantly struggle with God's guidelines for relationships. When the sense of being liked and loved by God is missing, we instinctively treat each other the way we deserve to be treated instead of the way Christ treats us. The cry you hear today in our society about "my rights" is simply a demand to treat people the way they deserve to be treated.

"What is wrong with that?" you might ask. There is a huge problem with that approach. In essence, it is the old "an eye for an eye and a tooth for a tooth" approach (see Matt. 5:38). The difficulty is that eventually everyone ends up toothless and blind! We impatiently end up demanding our rights, totally forgetting God's patience with us and his purpose for our life.

Ever had a struggle with being patient in your life? It was a huge hassle for me. However, once I caught a glimpse of how patient Christ had been with me, something changed within me. Once we get a three-dimensional picture with surround sound of God's patience within us, then we can whip our impatience problem in short order. That is why I have learned to ask Christ to frequently show me how patient He is with me, especially when I am uptight with someone.

If I lose sight of Christ's personal invitation to me, then I can easily find an excuse to be impatient with you. Oh, let me list the ways! It is even easier to find an excuse not to forgive you.

Forgiveness and Humility Lead to the Realization of God's Love for Us

I'm sure you also have noticed this: Most forgiving folks are ones who have hit the hard rocks of reality in life. They have learned to be patient in life. They have been to the bottom and they not only know how it feels, but they also know how gracious God is. They are humble folks. Humility is the pathway to intimacy with God:

> A man's pride will bring him low, but the humble in spirit will retain honor (Prov. 29:23, *NKJV*).

If we are humble, God will honor us. He will be intimate with us. And humility always involves a huge chunk of patience.

If we are proud and impatient and ignore His voice—like I did with my busyness—He will eventually deal with us at a distance. Humility is not seeing ourselves in comparison to others but in light of God's greatness. Remember, it usually takes time in the wilderness or at rock bottom for us to realize who we really are and just how profound God's love for us actually is.

THE KEY OF FORGIVENESS

Forgiveness is critical to the fulfillment of Christ's prayer for pure-hearted disciples. First of all, Paul pointed out we are imperfect people who constantly offend one another. I mean people can drive you crazy, especially if you are married to them. The main place discipleship is lived out is in the home, not at church. If it doesn't work at home, it will never work at church, because the home is the foundational unit of the Church. It was easier for the first-century believers to understand that, because they met in homes and didn't have church buildings.

During our weekend services recently we presented a painfully familiar picture through drama. A divorced couple was arguing with one another over what could have been and their dislike of one another. Having watched my mother go through seven divorces, the dialogue was very recognizable. I asked the congregation immediately after the drama, "If Robert and Joyce were your friends, what would you say to them? How would you help them out?"

The answers were predictable: They need to develop better communication skills. They need to listen to each other. They need to develop active listening skills. Now it is easy to understand why such suggestions came forth. When most couples are tangled in a serious conflict, they end up like my kids in the living room. They want to win and they feel hurt. In the process, the lines of communication begin to get overloaded with emotional static and then they shut down all together. You eventually end up with two toothless, blind and deaf people trying to communicate with each other out of their pain.

I pointed out to the listeners that day various research studies that have been done. The evidence is in and communication techniques like active listening don't work. Dr. Neil Jacobson found that even in the best-case scenarios there is only a 35 percent success rate with these approaches. Only 18 percent of the couples retain that success past one year.[3] At that point I could see eyebrows being raised all over the auditorium. People were thinking, *But wait a minute, Pastor Ted, don't we teach active-listening communication techniques in all our marriage enrichment classes and groups here at East Hill?* Reading their concerns I assured them we would continue to teach such helpful techniques. But I pointed out they will never work in a marriage until the critical first step is taken—forgiveness. Then and only then will active listening work.

Dr. John Gottman has done some fascinating work with understanding conflict in marriages. In fact, he is able to predict with over 90 percent accuracy whether or not a marriage will make it. Two discoveries in his research really turned on some lights for me. He discovered that most marital conflicts couldn't be resolved![4] I remember when this finally dawned on me. I was looking across the breakfast table at my wife thinking, *You know what, I'm never going to change this woman's mind. She is never going to see the light!* Once I accepted the fact that I could only change myself and not my spouse, our marriage started working a whole lot better. Now that doesn't mean we don't still work with all our heart at understanding one another and don't constantly try to develop better communication skills. But the bottom line is, we are not going to be able to just sit down with some new communication technique and resolve our differences. We always have to take the critical first step of forgiving one another and in the process learn to honor and respect each other, despite the fact we will never totally agree.

Dr. Gottman discovered another fact about marital conflict that really helped me in my struggles to love my wife. If I am ever going to be a pure-hearted disciple, I am called to love her as Christ loved the Church. At times that can be incredibly stressful. Dr. Gottman found out men are the weaker sex when it comes to verbal conflict.[5] It is a biological fact that men are more easily overwhelmed by marital conflict than their wife. The male cardiovascular system remains more reactive than the female and recovers from stress more slowly. Thus, in the middle of an argument, the female's biological readouts, such as blood pressure and pulse, are raised slightly, and the male's readings are through the roof.

That explained a great deal to me. I tend to be a fairly fearless guy, yet there are four words that strike terror in my soul. It is when my wife looks at me and says, "We need to talk." Send me into combat with a pellet gun. Have me fly a mission in downtown Baghdad with no wingman. Anything, but please, dear God, don't let me hear those words from my wife. Please not those words! It was so comforting to realize I wasn't the only man on the planet who had those responses, but it also told me why I could get so easily hurt in marital arguments. But I can just as easily hurt Diane by tuning her out. It is not that I don't love her; it is just that I don't want to fail. I am avoiding something that is highly stressful for me at times. Add to that the fact that most marital arguments are not solvable, and you realize you are never going to get to the party without the critical first step of forgiveness.

THE SON WHO MISSED THE PARTY

The story of the prodigal son is without a doubt my favorite parable that Christ told. However, most folks don't read the end of the story, so they miss the full impact of what Christ was getting at.

> Meanwhile, the older son was in the field. When he came near the house, he heard music and dancing. So he called one of the servants and asked him what was going on. "Your brother has come," he replied, "and your father has killed the fattened calf because he has him back safe and sound." The older brother became angry and refused to go in. So his father went out and pleaded with him. But he answered his father, "Look! All these years I've been slaving for you and never disobeyed your orders. Yet you never gave me even a young goat so I could celebrate with my friends. But when this son of yours who has squandered your property with prostitutes comes home, you kill the fattened calf for him!" "My son," the father said, "you are always with me, and everything I have is yours" (Luke 15:25-31).

There is nothing more tragic in life than to miss the party. The elder son understood his relationship with the father to be based on performance. That is why when it came to paying the price to attend the party—forgiving his father—he couldn't do it. Forgiveness is always the critical first step.

The younger son didn't have that problem. He came to his senses. He came clean. He came home to his father and experienced the father's forgiveness. As the father placed the robe, ring and sandals on the lost son, signifying his acceptance, the son felt forgiven.

Every now and then I will hear another church leader refer to our church as a garbage dump. "They let anyone in there," they will say. Or they declare, "Oh, the reason they have grown so much is only sick people go to East Hill." Someone asked me what I thought about such comments. I said I considered them compliments. At least we have sense enough to know we need help and forgiveness. Give me forgiven people over driven, angry elder-brother church folks any day! Folks who have truly felt God's forgiveness down in their soul will be able to do things they would never had been able to do otherwise.

Three weeks after I resigned from the military, I was in theological graduate school. Talk about a severe adjustment. Of course, I think it was more of an adjustment for the seminary folks who had to learn how to deal with me. Part of a class requirement was to serve at a local church. I found a church, went in to see the pastor and announced I was there to get the place squared away. Whatever he needed done, I would take care of it. He suggested I get together some greeters for the Sunday morning service—folks to welcome people as they came into the service. I asked the pastor when he wanted the greeters to be at the front door. Then I asked for a list of the names of people who could possibly serve and walked out the door announcing they would be in place at 0900 hours. I called them up, informing them they needed to have their shoes shined, hair cut and suits pressed and they needed to stand at attention as the people arrived. Would you believe not one greeter showed up? After a couple of weeks I was totally frustrated and went to see the pastor. I told him, "I can't believe these civilians. How do you get anything done around here?"

The gracious pastor simply said, "Son." I have since learned that when an elder in the faith starts his sentence with "Son," correction is on its way! He went on to say, "What do you want to happen? Have a couple people standing at the front of the church, or do you want to have something supernatural happen in people's lives?" I fell apart and began to cry. I saw how driven and self-centered I had been. But that is not the end of the story. The pastor came out from behind his desk, put his arms around me and tenderly declared, "Ted, someday you are going to be a great pastor." I will never forget that moment. He put the robe, ring and sandals on me that day. I felt forgiven to the depths of my being. He welcomed me to the party.

Forgiveness changes lives and it changes marriages. It is foundational to unity at home and in the Church. That is precisely why Jesus was so emphatic about its importance, even declaring you will not be forgiven unless you forgive (see Matt. 6:14-15). He was not saying that God is going to get you unless you forgive; instead, He is helping us understand that forgiveness is the power of God expressed in a fallen world. When you block forgiveness, you hinder the power of God in your life and relationships.

PRACTICAL TIPS ON FORGIVENESS

Take a deep breath, because I am not going end the chapter here. When I first started trying to attend church, it took me a while before I could hang in there. What drove me nuts were the YBH sermons. I would be told I needed to forgive people or I needed to do this or that to be a good Christian. Yet I would never be told how, other than to try harder. I called them "yes but how" sermons. I agreed I needed help, but all the speakers gave me was exhortation. Let me close by sharing several practical tips that have helped me in life. All of us carry baggage over the issue of forgiveness. If you are married, you are picking up baggage all the time. The difference between a good marriage and a troubled one is how we deal with the baggage.

Pay the Price

First and foremost, especially in a marriage, you will have to pay the price. To get to the celebration of marriage God has for you, or if you are single and desire healthy and fulfilling relationships, you will have to pay the price, not for your admission to the party, but for your mate's or friend's admission. After listening to scores of hurting people over the years, I have learned that hurting people hurt others. I am not excusing their behavior, but it helps me to not take their actions personally and end up so offended. However, at times it is appropriate for me to shoulder their hurt and to help pay their price into the party.

Often now a husband comes in to see me and pours out his hurt over his sexual relationship with his wife. "She rejects me at times sexually. I am not being pushy or insensitive, but she will just shove me away and that hurts, but then at other times she is responsive to me. I can't understand her and I'm getting bitter about it." Depending on which survey you read, 30 to 40 percent of women have been sexually abused in our society. I think the actual numbers are much higher. My point is that the husband may be dealing with a wife who has been sexually abused, and he has never connected the dots.

I will usually say to him, "Sir, when I asked you if your wife had ever been abused sexually and you said she had, you have the answer to your question. Don't react to her. Realize it is not just about you. Forgive her and don't play the sexual martyr. Instead, provide a safe and gracious environment for her to deal with her struggles. It is a lot like walking along a beach when the tide is out. You may see old tires, junk, whatever has been thrown into the water, but this is a picture of your wife's soul. She didn't throw the stuff in there. It was done to her. And if you are there for her each time the tide goes out in her life, eventually you can help her remove a tire, some junk or a painful memory. There will come a time when you will walk along a beautiful moonlit beach together and she will turn to you with tears in her eyes because you gave her a gift that no other man could." Sometimes we have to pay the price so that others can come to the party of God's grace and blessing.

Learn to Watch the White Line

Second, learn to watch the white line. At times those you love aren't the ones you need to forgive—you need to forgive those folks you can't stand. You hate them! In fact, you love to hate them! You hold imaginary conversations with them in your head and you always have the final word. You pull a verbal slam dunk on them in front of everyone and walk away smiling from ear to ear. You know what Christ calls you to do; but when you see them or have to deal with them, you end up spiritually running off the road. You want to feel good toward them—it seems totally impossible, but forgiveness is possible in Christ.

In the state of Oregon in which I live, you can run into a lot of logging trucks on the back roads. It is a real challenge to come to the top of a hill on a narrow one-and-a-half-lane road and encounter a logging truck coming the other way, especially late at night in the rain. Why? Because the truck always seems to have its headlights on high, aiming straight for your eyes. The natural tendency is for your eyes to be drawn toward the lights. But if they do, the consequences could be devastating, like joining the other bugs on the truck's radiator grill. How do you handle the challenge? You look for the white line that separates your lane from the shoulder. You keep your eyes focused on that line until the truck passes.

In the high beam of your emotions, you can't do anything about what the person did to you any more than you can turn down the lights of the truck. You have to learn at that moment that you can't fight an emotion with an emotion. You can't choose to feel forgiveness for the person no matter how many sermons you hear. Instead you have to dig down to a deeper motivation—your convictions. You have to look to the white line of your convictions. That is the only safe way through the struggle. In your emotions you can't stand the person, but your convictions are not controlled by your emotions. For me it sounds something like this, "Lord, in a bunker in the middle of a raging war I received your forgiveness. And I receive your forgiveness right now, no matter how I feel. I made a decision to follow a forgiving Christ and I am not about to change my mind."

Here is the interesting thing about the whole process. It is in those moments of high tension and emotional struggle that I frequently make an amazing discovery. It is there and uniquely there that I experience Christ's forgiveness. It is not during the times when everything is going well. When that pastor put his arms around me years ago and spoke about my capacity to become a great pastor, I experienced the forgiveness of God. The person I hadn't been able to forgive was myself. That is what I had been battling with for years. Yet in that moment I saw the line of God's love for me that had extended all the way back to the beginning of my life.

Start Where the Prodigal Son Did

Finally, realize you will usually start where the prodigal son did. The place to begin with forgiveness is always with you. It is a waste of time to hear a teaching or read a book about forgiveness and then go out and try to repair relationships. Don't try to change anyone else until you have let God change you with His staggering power of forgiveness. Once you let God change you, then you see other people with new eyes. The elder brother never got to the party as far as we know. He couldn't pay the price of admission—forgiving his brother. Usually we can't either, but Christ has already paid for our admission, which is a truth we discover at even greater depth as we walk with Christ through the years.

> *Don't try to change anyone else until you have let God change you with His staggering power of forgiveness.*

FINAL THOUGHTS

You have probably noticed this but it still shocks me: The closer I get to Christ, the more I realize how messed up I really am. It is a disconcerting process. Just about the time I think I am finally getting it together, Jesus will point out this character stain on my soul. It is a spot I have never seen before. In the light of His presence, I begin to notice things about myself that used to escape my attention. I feel like I am standing at a party and there is this huge stain running down the front of my shirt. Everyone is looking at me and I feel really dumb. That is when Jesus comes and enfolds me in His strong arms of acceptance, forgiveness and love. Forgiveness is deeply experienced once again, but this time at a deeper dimension of my soul.

It is in this incredible experience of coming back to the place of the prodigal son or daughter time and again that we are uniquely discipled into Christ's character. My deepest prayer for you is that you would constantly come home to the Father and know His forgiveness at ever-deeper dimensions of your life, because the forgiveness of God is the power of God on display in our fallen world. His forgiveness unifies believers and serves as a witness to the world.

Let's look at how you are doing with respect to the issue that ties it all together—unity. Read each question and circle the number that best corresponds to your answer.

1. Have you heard Christ's personal invitation of gracious acceptance to you?

Not really		I think so		Profoundly
1	2	3	4	5

2. Do you believe Christ actually likes you?

No, to be honest, I don't		Not sure at times		Yes, indeed
1	2	3	4	5

3. Do you tend to treat people the way you think they deserve to be treated, especially when you are upset with them?

Usually		Occasionally		Normally, not
1	2	3	4	5

4. How patient are you in life?

Not very		Sometimes patient		Very patient
1	2	3	4	5

5. How "praus" are you in the tough times of life? When the pressure is on, do you tend to be self-controlled?

It's really hard for me		I can lose it at times		Usually
1	2	3	4	5

6. How forgiving would your mate or friends say you are?

Not really		Moderately		Always forgiving
1	2	3	4	5

7. How easy is it for you to pay the price for others, to help them process their pain in life?

It's very difficult for me		At times I carry the load		I love doing it
1	2	3	4	5

8. How hard is it for you to ignore your emotions when someone has deeply hurt you and instead respond out of your convictions?

A real struggle		I battle at times		I can stay focused
1	2	3	4	5

9. When is the last time Christ revealed to you an area in your life that you didn't know was messed up?

Never		It's happened a couple of times		How about this week!
1	2	3	4	5

10. Have you really felt God's forgiveness in your life?

Not really		A little bit		At times I am overwhelmed by it
1	2	3	4	5

Score _____ (Add together the numbers you circled.)

Enter this score for Unity in the appropriate space on the Discipleship Development Analysis Tool in chapter 12.

CHAPTER TWELVE

WELCOME TO SAINT PETER'S CLUB

Deciding to Grow in Christ

And that You love them as much as You love Me.
(SEE JOHN 17:23.)

Please enter all of the scores you received from the evaluations at the end of chapters 3-11 on the appropriate line of the Discipleship Development Analysis Tool located on the next page.

DISCIPLESHIP DEVELOPMENT ANALYSIS TOOL

Total score for Joy _____ x 2 = _____ Final score
from chapters 3-4

Total score for Holiness _____ x 2 = _____ Final
score from chapter 5

Total score for Grace _____ x 2 = _____ Final score
from chapters 6-7

Total score for Truth _____ x 2 = _____ Final score
from chapters 8-9

Total score for Vision _____ x 2 = _____ Final score
from chapter 10

Total score for Unity _____ x 2 = _____ Final score
from chapter 11

Take your final score in each category and enter the results on the Discipleship Development Analysis Chart on the appropriate radial arm (see p. 228). After entering the final score in each category, connect the results to see how balanced your growth is and if there are any flat spots.

Here are some guidelines for evaluating your score:

If you scored between 20-40, this is an area where the Holy Spirit is working deeply in your life. How can you more

DISCIPLESHIP DEVELOPMENT ANALYSIS CHART

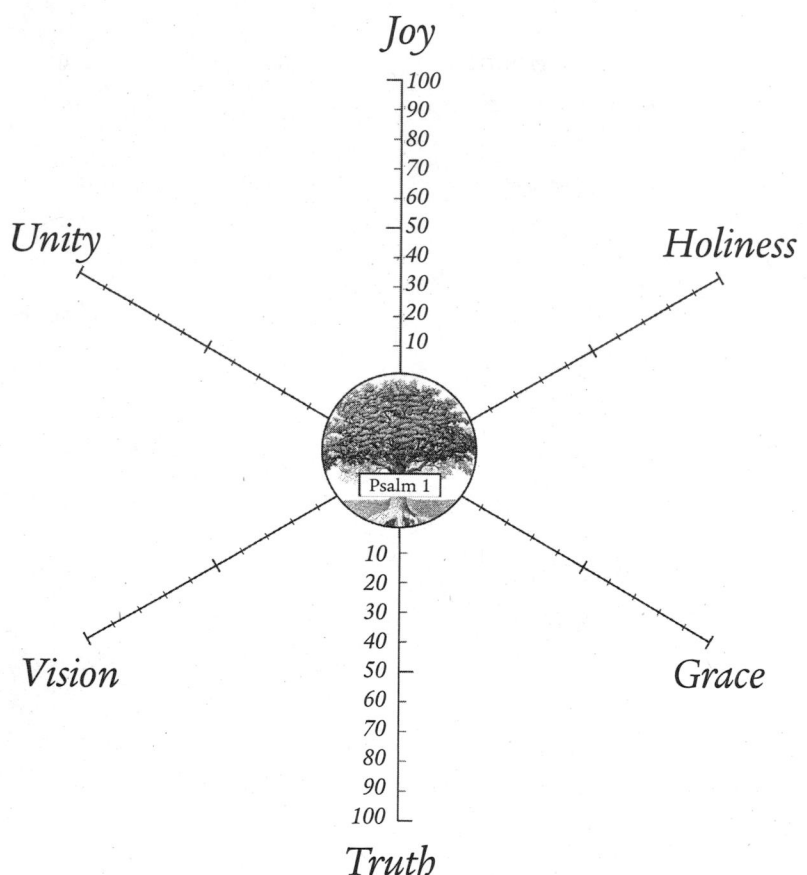

effectively cooperate with Him?

If you scored between 40-60, there is growth in this area of your life. How can you increase that growth?

If you scored between 60-80, there is significant growth in this area. How can you reach a level of excellence that would deeply honor God?

If you scored between 80-100, you are doing well. How about finding a new way to celebrate God's goodness in your life! Throw a party!

THE OUTRAGEOUS LOVE OF JESUS

After completing your Discipleship Development Analysis, I would like to officially invite you to become a charter member in the Saint Peter's Club. The only qualification is that you didn't score a perfect 100 in all six areas and that you have decided to follow Christ. Congratulations! You qualify!

There is still an aspect of Christ's discipleship prayer for us we haven't focused on yet—His personal love for us. Not our love for Him, because our love isn't that amazing. It is often fickle, fleeting and just plain foolish. The one thing that ultimately makes discipleship possible is Christ's outrageous, incomprehensible and divine love for us. Let's look at that awesome love for a second before we address the practical aspects of your analysis results.

Every now and then I find myself standing in amazement when I remember where I spiritually came from. It has become abundantly clear that I am where I am today courtesy of God's grace—His love for me.

Through the years, my prayers have cleaned up a bit from my military days. I have a better grasp on the Bible. After getting a doctorate, I learned where the sacred cows are located. Yet I still end up running over them with a disturbing frequency. At times I don't feel like I fit in, and I still can say some really dumb things. If you are like me and didn't max out the Discipleship Development Analysis, then welcome to the Saint Peter's Club. It is an unofficial group of folks who struggle at times with getting it right, who every now and then really get upset with themselves and feel like throwing in the towel. They have a heart for God but frequently end up stumbling over their own best intentions.

> *The one thing that ultimately makes discipleship possible is Christ's outrageous, incomprehensible and divine love for us.*

There is a passage in God's love letters to us—John 21—that is especially precious to club members. Peter has thrown in the towel. He has gone fishing with his friends. They have fished all night but caught nothing. Jesus is standing on the shoreline as they return and asks them if they have caught anything. They tell him the truth, which is one of the greatest miracles in the entire Bible—fishermen can make golfers look honest. During breakfast, Jesus asks Peter three times if he loves Him. A lot of folks totally miss what is going on here. They say things like, "Well, Jesus was just reminding Peter of the three times he had denied Him." *Wrong God!* Jesus never treats those He loves like that. Others say, "Jesus was reminding Peter of His love for him despite his failures." That commentary is better, but something much more profound is taking place.

My wife is Jewish, so it is almost a requirement that we watch the movie *Fiddler on the Roof* at least once a year. Because I love her, I don't mind. There is a scene in the movie that is mandatory for all Saint Peter's Club members to see. Tevye, a poor Jewish dairyman in Russia, is having a stressful day. His daughters are getting married to some pretty strange guys. The communists are taking over, and soon his entire village will be driven off their land. Tevye goes to his wife, Golde, and asks her, "Do you love me?" (By the way, they have a contract marriage that was arranged by their parents.) She reacts to the question, "I am your wife. What do you mean do I love you? I cooked your meals, cleaned your house and bore you children. You are a fool!" To which he responds, "I know. But do you love me?" And she pauses, thinking over the 25 years of victories and struggles, 25 years of sharing the same house and same bed, and then she responds, "If that is not love, then I don't know what it is." Tevye, like an excited kid, says, "Then you love me!" They sit down on their bed and sing, "After 25 years it is nice to know you love me." But it is not just nice to know. It touches their hearts so deeply that they can hardly look at one another. Therefore, my closing question is simply, Who is the vulnerable one when Christ asks, "Peter, do you love Me?" *It was Jesus!* Despite all of Peter's failures and foibles, even after he threw in the towel, Christ reaches out to him with staggering vulnerability.

OUR VERY BEST RESPONSE TO SUCH LOVE

We can't give up! We can't quit! His love demands our all—our very best! That is the Jesus we serve in the royal order of the Saint Peter's Club. "Ted, how should I respond to those areas where I am kind of flat spiritually?" you ask. Well, great question. Most of our graphs look like a flat tire at some point—great in some areas and deflated in others. Discipleship is about two things once we make the commitment to really grow in Christ because of our love for Him. First of all, it is about balance. The flat spot or spots in your life are preventing you from picking up speed spiritually. You can't get rolling. Don't ignore the flat spots, or you will stay stuck in life. Remember, your spiritual health affects every area of your life, especially your closest relationships. One of the most energizing things you can do for your marriage and for your kids is to begin to grow spiritually.

Second, discipleship is about continual growth. The influence of Christ in our life should be ever increasing until the day we die—much like a healthy tree generates rings of growth as it matures. The last thing you should do is take your chart and compare it with anyone else's. You are a unique creation of God, and the dimensions of your growth circle in relationship to someone else are irrelevant. We all experience seasons of growth and right now you may be going through a dry time. A healthy tree in the middle of a dry season will not have rapidly expanding growth rings, but it will be sending its roots deeper into the soil. And that is crucial, because without those dry times of driving the roots of our life deeper into Christ, the winds of adversity will eventually topple us. You will never be able to handle the hurricanes of hell apart from those dry times. That is why we need to learn to cherish them. I know, I can't stand them either, but by faith I have learned to treasure them. And when the rains of the anointing presence of the Holy Spirit fall afresh, the depth and balance of growth in our life not only bring joy to the heart of God but also a profound sense of fulfillment to our soul, because our life begins to have a greater impact in this needy world.

Let me suggest six practical ways to respond to your analysis. I have constructed the steps into an acrostic—GROWTH—so that they will be easy to remember in the frantic pace of our daily lives.

Give Thanks

Often when I begin walking through a psychological analysis with an individual in the counseling office, the air is filled with tension. Whenever I sense anxiety, I stop the process and attempt to put what is occurring into perspective. I may say something like "You know, it is never easy to see ourselves when we are not at our best. Nearly all of us feel threatened or frustrated. But there is another way to look at this information. The analysis can either be a healing scalpel or a wounding knife. Christ, however, always brings truth into our life to heal us, not hurt us. So let's look at this analysis from His perspective."

Then I point out to them that this information is not new data to God. He knows us far better than we know ourselves. In fact, this analysis gives us marvelous insight into where the Holy Spirit has been trying to work in our life. While we may have been feeling pain and wondering what God was doing, we don't have to guess anymore—the areas of our personal needs are clearly identified. This provides us with an unprecedented opportunity to cooperate with what God is doing in our soul. Then I invite them to take a moment or two and lift thanks to God for this information. This could be a stepping-stone into a deeper relationship with God and their loved ones.

Why don't *you* take a moment and lift praise to God for this opportunity to cooperate at a deeper level with His healing and maturing process in your life. Revelation of personal need is never a negative thing in life. It only becomes negative when your pride or need to appear as if you have it all together gets in the way.

Risk Opening Up Your Heart Deeply to God in Prayer

The Discipleship Development Analysis is obviously not a scientific survey. And that is fine, because I am talking about the battles of your soul, not some academic debate. Therefore, the effectiveness and power of the analysis are directly connected to prayer. If the chart can aid you visually in your prayers, then it can have a *huge* impact in your life.

When you pray, picture that flat spot or spots in your soul and ask God the Holy Spirit to open your spiritual eyes. Ask for understanding to know if that is an area where you have been wounded or just an area where you need to grow. Jesus is the great physician and the master psychologist. He and He alone knows the intricacies of your soul and, just as important, the ultimate calling of God in your life. He and He alone brings to your life not just healing but also a profound sense of fulfillment. He and He alone brings the effulgent flow of God the Father's richest blessing in your life.

Christ's rule in your life is never Machiavellian but absolutely marvelous. May I recommend you take the next 30 days and simply ask God to open your spiritual eyes to the depth of the need you have within. Allow God the Holy Spirit to penetrate the depths of your being as you lift up your need for growth in this area of your life. It will take a deep discipline of your soul to do this on a daily basis for a month, because we tend to pray about immediate problems and perceived needs. Our perception of what our real needs are is frequently clouded by our well-developed denial mechanisms. As you pray over the area or areas of need, make sure to journal what you are sensing from the Lord. Write it all down. Don't try to analyze it; just work at developing your ability to write what you think you are hearing from the Lord. After the 30 days of prayer are over, take what you have written and meet with a mentor—someone you trust, someone who is further down the road spiritually than you are—and talk through what have experienced.

It is critical that you don't attempt to self-evaluate what you have written down; otherwise the experience will become one of spiritual navel-gazing and self-absorption rather than personal growth. Discipleship is never a journey you take alone. You will need encouragers, evaluators and fellow travelers to speak faith, hope and wisdom into your soul in this lifelong process.

Observe How Important This Issue Is to God and to Others
This part of the process can be very challenging. But I am convinced this is the major piece missing in believers' lives today. Without this step, you will lack the resolve and motivation to persevere in the healing and growth process.

Isaiah, the Old Testament prophet, had blasted the people of Israel for years over their sinfulness before he came to a new place in his life (see Isa. 6). In the midst of a personal crisis, this magnificent prophet saw the truth about himself and how his own sinfulness affected God and others. He declares, "I am ruined, destroyed, wiped out" (see Isa. 6:5). No sooner had Isaiah declared his inabilities than God started proclaiming His abilities through him.

Take a honest look at your weaknesses and wounds never results in condemnation in God's presence; instead, it releases His power in your life. That is precisely why reviewing what God has said to you about your weak areas, the areas where you need growth, is so important. And it is something you can never do alone. Time and again, as I have reviewed my struggles with a spiritual mentor or friend, at some point I find myself in the manifest presence of God. Suddenly, I see how my actions have affected others and why they are so upsetting—how what I said to my wife hurt her so deeply, how what I did wounded the hearts of my kids. Sure, it is never a fun experience, but it transforms your whole motivational basis in that relationship. You don't feel beat up. What beats you up is when people you love react negatively to you and you can't understand why. But once you see what is going on from their perspective, it changes everything. I think that is exactly what happened in Isaiah's life. God was asking, "Whom shall I send? And who will go for us?" (Isa. 6:8). Isaiah starts jumping up and down saying, "Here am I. Send me!" (Isa. 6:8).

Isaiah was ready to throw in the towel just a few chapters before. He was tired of putting up with the hard-hearted people and their negative reactions toward him. Yet, not long after, he is leaning forward, just waiting for the opportunity to give it another shot. Once you see your weaknesses from God's perspective and through the eyes of those nearest to you, it changes everything! Being a pure-hearted disciple is no longer an option! It is a necessity!

> *Once you see your weaknesses from God's perspective and through the eyes of those nearest to you, it changes everything!*

Widen Your Understanding

Discipleship—in-depth spiritual growth—is not simply a process of learning basic doctrinal truths of the faith. Nor is it just the acquiring of certain relational skills. It is a supernatural process of becoming uniquely *you* in Christ. Not "uniquely you" as the world uses the term today. It is not an extended process of self-fulfillment into eternity. But on the other hand, it is not self-annihilation where Christ is everything and we cease to exist—that is Buddhism by another name.

Far greater authors than I have written numerous learned tomes about the spiritual-growth process. One of the things I have learned through the years is that my growth is always in direct proportion to how I handle my struggles in life. Significant growth usually doesn't take place when everything is going my way. Instead, it happens when all hell is breaking loose and I am struggling to keep my head, heart and soul above water.

Yet when I trust God's promises to keep me afloat in the storm, I don't just stay alive. I look back and realize significant spiritual development has taken place. Thus, I have learned to widen my understanding of the growth process. When I apply God's Word at specific points of my need—understanding how important the problem is to God and others—it is there and uniquely there that major maturation takes place. Paul makes this phenomena clear in 2 Corinthians 10:5:

> We demolish arguments and every pretension that sets itself up against the knowledge of God, and we take captive every thought to make it obedient to Christ.

The Greek word for "to take captive"—*airchmalotizo*—literally means "to take one captive with a sword or spear, to bring into subjection."[1] The context of Paul's comments deals with the challenging issue of spiritual warfare. In the journey of pursuing Christ as a pure-hearted disciple, it is a given that spiritual warfare is going to be a *huge* issue. There is absolutely no way you are ever going to win the battle over those spiritually flat areas of your life simply by trying harder. The sword of God's Word must be brought to bear on those specific areas in your life where you really want to grow. The flat spot or spots in your life are not going to turn around easily, because hell has a vested interest in seeing you struggle for the rest of your life. Once you begin to aggressively move into becoming a pure-hearted disciple, you are Satan's worst nightmare. You begin to walk in a joy he can't pull down and a holiness he can't pollute; a grace he can't understand and a truth he can't stand. Your life reflects a vision he hates and a unity that devastates him.

That is precisely why you need to clearly identify your weaknesses and areas where you need growth. Then search God's Word for His promise to you at those specific points of need. Don't stop there; take the next step. Absorb God's eternal, awesome Word. Memorize it and bring it to bear on the flat spots of your spiritual life. When you do that, hell's strongholds will begin to fold in your life.

Treasure Accountability

This is the most practical part of the process and the most relationally challenging. If you are ever going to totally shatter hell's strongholds in your life, if you are ever going to see the Holy Spirit supernaturally revive the flat spots in your life, you have to treasure accountability. There needs to be someone in your life who knows all of your secrets. We are only as sick as our secrets. The person needs to not only know your secrets but also love you enough to not let you stay the same.

You need someone in your life who can encourage you and challenge you at the same time, an individual you can develop growth plans with and a friend who will be a reference point for you. If you decide you are going to get a handle on your eating, sex life, spending habits, Bible study practices or whatever, this person will hold your heart to the healing fires of God's grace. The individual will hold you accountable. They don't heal you—God does, but the person loves you enough to ask you if you are really changing. Did you stick with the budget this week? Did you eat healthily this week? Did you avoid looking at Internet pornography this week?

Cry out to God for such a treasure in your life—a person who will hold you accountable, a person you can dream with concerning your future, a person you can develop battle plans with. Once you have such a person in your life, treasure them. I mean treasure them!

Hold On to the Dream God Has Placed in Your Heart

The major difference between a river and a swamp is the river is going one place while the swamp tries to go everywhere. The river has a goal—an objective. It is determined to reach the sea. The swamp, however, rebels against the discipline of the riverbanks and constantly remains an underachiever. Sure, they cover a lot of ground but not with any depth. Let the high-alpine beauty of a God-vision bring crystal clarity to your soul. And be about one thing—becoming a pure-hearted disciple of Jesus Christ.

FINAL THOUGHTS

My prayer for you is that on this journey called discipleship you would catch just a glimpse of what a treasure you are to God. All it takes is a glimpse. That truth changes everything. It gives the struggles of this life meaning. My children are grown now and have kids of their own, but there are moments when I look at them and my heart is overwhelmed by how much I love them. And every time it happens, Father God always says to me, "Ted, it's not even close to the depth of love I have for you." And God the Father is speaking of His profound love for you every day as well. Pure discipleship is just learning how to live and walk in light of the fact that you are so loved by God.

Study Guide

Each of these short studies is designed not only to interact with the concepts presented in *Living Life Boldly* but also to point the reader back to Scripture as the ultimate source of those concepts.

The questions presented here will help the reader dig a little deeper into the biblical background of Christ's prayer for His present-day disciples—John 17. The six critical axes of a disciple's life—joy, holiness, grace, truth, vision and unity—are rooted in the full revelation of Scripture, not just in one prayer. Christ, the Word, prayed for us from the total depths of God's Word.

Chapters Three and Four: The Beauty of Joy

[Joy is] something too near to see, too plain to be
understood, on this side of knowledge.

C. S. LEWIS

The Talmud (a Jewish commentary on the Old Testament) says Adam and Eve did not know what darkness was until they were driven out of paradise. As the sun began to set, they were filled with fear. When all grew dark, they fell to the earth in silent despair, thinking God had withdrawn the light forever. But when the first beam appeared over the eastern hills, drying their tears, they cried out, "Weeping may endure for a night, but joy cometh in the morning" (Ps. 30:5, *KJV*).

1. How does the concept of joy relate to God's character?

Read Deuteronomy 28:63; Jeremiah 32:41; Luke 15:20-32.

2. Who is ultimately the source of our joy? Read Psalm 45:7; Romans 15:13.

3. How do we find joy in such a painful world? Read Luke 21:28; Philippians 4:4.

4. Joy can be based on circumstances or on something of a higher value. On which of these is a deeper type of joy based? Read Psalm 4:7-8.

5. Paul has a threefold foundation to his joy. What are the three aspects of his understanding of joy? For the first aspect, read Philippians 2:2, 1 Thessalonians 2:19. For the second aspect, read 2 Corinthians 6:10; Colossians 1:24. For the third aspect, read Galatians 5:22.

Paul's life so graphically displays the beauty of biblical joy. This kind of joy is found in amazing places. God's joy tells us of His beauty in the midst of a fallen world.

Chapter Five: The Harbor of Holiness

When the Emperor arrested Chrysostom (an Early Church leader) and tried to make him recant his faith, he shook his head. The Emperor said to his guards, "Throw him in prison." "No," said one of them, "he will be glad to go, for he delights in the presence of his God in quiet!"
"Well, execute him," said the Emperor. "He will be glad to die," said the soldier, "for he wants to go to heaven; I heard him say so the other day." "There is only one thing that can give Chrysostom pain, and that is, to make him sin; he said he was afraid of nothing but sin. If you can make him sin, you will make him unhappy."
WILLIAM NORTON

1. The basic meaning of holiness appears early in the Old Testament and refers to what? Read Exodus 3:5; 19:6.

2. Holiness has been referred to as the characteristic that embraces every distinctive attribute of the Godhead—the Trinity. As a sunbeam is a combination of all the colors of the spectrum, so holiness is the manifestation of all the attributes of God. Why would someone say that? Read 1 Samuel 2:2; Habakkuk 1:13; John 17:11; Acts 2:4; 4:30.

3. The progressive revelation of Scripture in the New Testament moves the concept of holiness from what is on the outside to what is on the inside and takes on a very personal focus. Who became the focus? Read Hebrews 12:10.

4. Christ is our standard and our safe harbor. How does this apply to our living a holy life? Read Hebrews 2:11.

5. Why would Chrysostom be so afraid of purposefully walking in sin? How long do our decisions concerning holiness live with us? Read Revelation 22:11.

Chapters Six and Seven: The Goodness of God's Grace

When I get to heaven, I shall see three wonders there: the first wonder will be to see so many people there whom I did not expect to see; the second, to miss many people whom I did expect to see; and the third and greatest wonder of all will be to find myself there.

JOHN NEWTON

1. Some see a severe difference between the Old Testament and the New Testament with regard to grace. They say grace is not mentioned that much in the Old Testament. Is that true? Read Genesis 6:8-9; Exodus 33:11-12; Joshua 1:5; 1 Kings 6:13; Psalm 149:4; Isaiah 54:8; Hosea 14:4; Zephaniah 3:17.

2. Grace is God's kindness and love shown to us, even though we do not deserve it. In the New Testament, God's grace took a radical step forward. How would you say grace changed from the Old Testament to the New Testament? Compare Nehemiah 9:28-31 with Hebrews 4:14-16.

3. What is our part as New Testament disciples with respect to grace? How would you sum it up in one word? Read Philippians 3:12-15; Colossians 1:10-11; 2 Thessalonians 1:3; Hebrews 6:1; 2 Peter 3:18.

4. Is this growth automatic or is it possible to misuse God's grace? Read Galatians 5:4; Jude 4.

5. How can we be assured that we will be pleasantly surprised like John Newton was when we leave this life? Read Jude 24; Revelation 3:10.

Chapters Eight and Nine: The Anchor of Truth

In my youth, science was more important to me than either man or God. I worshiped science. Its advance had surpassed man's wildest dreams. It took many years for me to discover that science, with all its brilliance, lights only a middle chapter of creation. I saw the aircraft I love destroying the civilization I expected it to save. Now I understand that spiritual truth is more essential to a nation than the mortar in its city walls. For when the actions of a people are undergirded by spiritual truths, there is safety. When spiritual truths

are rejected, it is only a matter of time before civilization will collapse.
We must understand spiritual truths and apply them to our modern life.
We must draw strength from the almost forgotten virtues of
simplicity, humility, contemplation and prayer. It requires a
dedication beyond science, beyond self, but the rewards are
great and it is our only hope.

CHARLES LINDBERGH

1. In the Old Testament, the concept of truth has a twofold focus. What are these two focal points? For the first point, read Deuteronomy 17:4; 1 Kings 10:6. For the second point, read Genesis 42:16; Deuteronomy 32:4.

2. The ultimate definition of truth is deeply personal and relates to one person. Who is that? Read Psalms 96:13; 119:89.

3. Our response to God and His Law is to carry a specific character trait in our innermost being. How are we to show that response? Read Psalm 51:6; Ephesians 5:8-9.

4. With the tendency that all of us have to deny the truth, how is it possible to sustain that response? Read John 14:6-14; 16:12-15.

5. Coca-Cola claims to be the real thing. But who is the real thing? Read John 4:23; 6:32,35; Hebrews 8:2.

Chapter Ten: The Wings of Vision

The poorest man is not he who is without a cent, but he
who is without a dream.

PENNSYLVANIA SCHOOL JOURNAL

1. Is a sense of vision in a believer's life an option or something reserved only for the "spiritual elite"? Read Proverbs 29:18; Acts 2:14-18.

2. What or who should be the source of our sense of vision in life? Read Acts 13:2; 16:9-10; 20:22.

3. Why is vision such a critical part of spiritual leadership? Read Nehemiah 2:17-18; Acts 7:55-56; 9:3-6; 10:9-23.

4. How does vision not only provide us with the ability to motivate others, withstand adversity and understand what we were created for but also provide a kind of perspective in our life despite our failures? Read Acts 13:36-37; 26:19.

Chapter Eleven: The High Calling of Unity

A weary traveler arrived at the French village of Doubs on Sunday evening at twilight, and found people hurrying throughout the streets to church, each carrying a lamp. A villager explained: "We have no other way of lighting the church. In 1550 when the church was built, the mayor of the village decided that each member should bring his own lamp. Everyone goes there to make it brighter, for he knows that if he stays away, the church will be darker." When he entered the church, the traveler saw that on every pew was a place for a lighted lamp, and as the church gradually filled, the cumulative effect of the multitude of lighted lamps was startling. The whole building was illuminated with a soft radiance, indescribably beautiful and impressive.

AL BRYANT

1. Does God view unity among believers as something beautiful or as something benign? Read Psalm 133; Acts 2:1-4,40-43.

2. What are some of the most common barriers to unity? Read Genesis 13:7-8; Galatians 5:14-15; Ephesians 4:25.

3. What enables us to reach the high calling of unity God purposed for us? Read Nehemiah 4:16-18; John 6:53-58; Acts 2:38-39; 1 Corinthians 12:13; 1 John 2:7-11.

4. What is the ultimate expression of our unity—an expression that extends beyond time? Read Revelation 21:1-4.

5. What efforts are you presently involved in that will enable you to be prepared for the lamp-transcending experience (see Rev. 21:22-25)? What conscious choices are you making in your life right now to respond to Paul's challenge in Ephesians 4:1-6?

ENDNOTES

Chapter One

1. George Barna, *Re-churching the Unchurched* (Ventura, CA: Issachar Resources, 2000), p. 15.
2. Ibid., p. 15.
3. Ibid., p. 71.
4. Kent R. Hunter, *Move Your Church to Action* (Nashville, TN: Abingdon Press, 2000), p. 12.
5. Thomas T. Clegg and Warren Bird, *Lost in America* (Loveland, CO: Group Publishing, 2001), p. 25.
6. George Barna, *Growing True Disciples* (Ventura, CA: Issachar Resources, 2000), p. 60.
7. Andy Butcher, "Shock Study Reveals Christians More Likely to Divorce Than Non-Christians," *Charisma News Service*, December 23, 1999. http://www.charismanews.com/a.php?ArticleID=3074 (accessed August 27, 2003).
8. Clegg and Bird, *Lost in America*, p. 35.
9. Gustav Niebuhr, "The Church and the Challenge of Contemporary American Culture" (lecture at Calvin College, Grand Rapids, MI, January 8, 1999).
10. Justin D. Long, "North America: Decline and Fall of World Religions, 1900-2025," Global Evangelization Movement's Monday Morning Reality Check, no. 5, 1998. http://www.gem-werc.org/mmrc/mmrc9805.htm (accessed August 28, 2003).
11. Ibid.
12. Shelby Oppel, "Taking Their Faith to the Masses," *The Oregonian*, September 18, 2002.
13. J. Heinrich Arnold, *Discipleship: Living for Christ in the Daily Grind* (Farmington, PA: Plough Publishing House, 1994), n.p.
14. Mother Teresa, *Mother Teresa: Contemplative in the Heart of the World* (Ann Arbor, MI: Servant Books, 1985), p. 29.
15. Ibid.

Chapter Two

1. C. S. Lewis, *The Weight of Glory* (New York: Macmillan Publishers, 1965), pp. 3-4.
2. George Barna, *Growing True Disciples* (Ventura, CA: Issachar Resources, 2000), p. 70.

3. John Gillespie Magee, Jr., "High Flight," *Great Aviation Quotes.* http://www.skygod.com/quotes/highflight.html (accessed August 28, 2003).

Chapter Four

1. Kenneth S. Wuest, *Wuest's Word Studies,* vol. 2 (Grand Rapids, MI: Eerdmans Publishing, 1966), p. 94.
2. Source unknown.

Chapter Five

1. Neil McAleer, *The Cosmic Mind-Boggling Book* (New York: Warner Books, 1992), p. 142.
2. Robert Jastrow, *God and the Astronomers* (New York: W. W. Norton and Company, 1979), p. 116.
3. S. Allsop, B. Saunders, M. Phillips, and A. Carr, "A Trial of Relapse Prevention with Severely Dependent Problem Drinkers," *Addiction,* vol. 11 (1992), pp. 61-74.
4. Ted Roberts, *Pure Desire* (Ventura, CA: Regal Books, 1999), pp. 69-72.
5. Hans von Campenhausen, *The Fathers of the Church* (Peabody, MA: Hendrickson, 1998), n.p.
6. Dr. Leis Judd, quoted in Marcus Buckingham and Curt Coffman, *First Break All the Rules* (New York: Simon and Schuster, 1999), p. 80.
7. Douglas Weiss, *Good Enough to Wait* (Fort Worth, TX: Discovery Press, 2000), n.p.
8. Daniel G. Amen, *Change Your Brain: Change Your Life* (New York: Three River Press, 1998), n.p.
9. Ronald A. Ruden, *The Craving Brain: The Biobalance Approach to Controlling Addictions* (New York: HarperCollins Publishers, 1997), n.p.

Chapter Six

1. Dr. Daniel Brown, "Heroes of the Faith," D. L. Moody lecture series, vol. 3 (1999).
2. Ibid.
3. Alpha groups are a ministry designed to help unchurched individuals understand the basics of Christianity.

Chapter Seven

1. Source unknown.
2. Ivars Peterson, "Beyond the Top: Now That Physicists Have Found the Top Quark What's Next?" *Science News*, vol. 148 (1995), pp. 10-12.
3. Ralph Earle and Joseph H. Mayfield, *John—Acts*, vol. 7 of *Beacon Bible Commentary Series* (Kansas City, MO: Beacon Hill Press, 1965), p. 428.

Chapter Eight

1. *Meridian (Mississippi) Star*, n.d.
2. Andrew W. Blackwood, Jr., *Ezekiel: Prophecy of Hope* (Grand Rapids, MI: Baker Book House, 1965), p. 21.

Chapter Ten

1. Helen Keller, quoted in John Maxwell, "The Value of Vision," audio-cassette 4 of *Vision: The Process of Passing It On!* (El Cajon, CA: Injoy Ministries, n.d.).
2. George Barna, *Without a Vision the People Perish* (Glendale, CA: Barna Research Group, Ltd., 1991), n.p.
3. Paul Virilio, *Art and Fear*, trans. Julie Rose (New York: Continuum Publishing Group, 2000), n.p.

Chapter Eleven

1. Spiros Zodhiates, *The Hebrew-Greek Key Study Bible* (Chattanooga, TN: AMG Publishers, 1996), p. 1636.
2. Ibid., n.p.
3. Dr. Neil Jacobson, quoted in John M. Gottman, *The Seven Principles for Making a Marriage Work* (New York: Three Rivers Press, 1999), p. 10.
4. Ibid., p. 23.
5. Ibid., p. 38.

Chapter Twelve

1. Fritz Riennecker and Cleon Rogers, *Linguistic Key to the Greek New Testament* (Grand Rapids, MI: Zondervan Publishing House, 1982), p. 486.